HEART
AND SOUL

Personal Recollections of Life in the Police Force

HEART AND SOUL

BARRY DICKINS

Hardie Grant Books

Published in 2000
by Hardie Grant Books
12 Claremont St
South Yarra 3141

National Library of Australia Cataloguing-in-Publication Data:
Heart and Soul: personal recollections of life in the police force

ISBN 1 86498 077 X

1. Police – Australia. I. Dickins, Barry, 1949-.

363.20994

Cover and text design by David Rosemeyer
Typeset by J&M Typesetting
Produced by Griffin Press in Australia

To Mrs Jean Koch, widow of Ray Koch – shot in a hold-up at Heathcote, Victoria – and to Police Legacy

Acknowledgements

Honest talks for this book would not have surfaced without considerable and endless help. I thank Shirley Hardy-Rix for putting me in touch with Colleen Woolley; Gary Presland, vice-president of the Victoria Police Historical Society, for his interest and suggestions; Meg Galpin, secretary of Police Legacy, for introducing me to police widows Leeanne Holmes and Jean Koch; Mrs Pam Chessell for introducing me to Charles Pilgrim, her father; Sandy Grant, my publisher, for ideas, interest and suggestions; Tracy O'Shaughnessy, commissioning editor at Hardie Grant, for solidarity; Ben Ellis and Anna Lozynski for transcribing many of the interviews from audio tape; and Sally Moss, my editor, for pruning the text properly, and pruning me mercifully.

Special thanks to Robert Haldane for his foreword; and to Brian Hodge and Peter Free of the Police Historical Unit.

Also thanks to Rob Burns of the PTC Investigation Section for the photograph of Charles Pilgrim.

Foreword

Policing in Australia as we know it had its genesis with the arrival of the white invaders in 1788. Before that time social order was maintained without recourse to guns, uniforms or written regulations. European-style policing first began in Victoria in 1836 and the Victoria Police Force began as an entity in 1853.

Since that time more than 30,000 men and women – mostly men – have passed through the ranks of the Victoria Police, with more than 10,000 still serving in the year 2000.

Much has been written about famous crimes, criminals and the deeds of the infamous, such as Ned Kelly and John Wren, but precious little has been written about the lives – and feelings – of the upholders of law and order: 'the coppers'.

Some years ago, noted criminologists Duncan Chappell and Paul Wilson lamented the lack of published material about police in Australia and noted the fruitful fields of study yet to be pursued. In 1986 I added my voice to that chorus, highlighting the untold stories and personal reminiscences 'of thousands of police – men and women, serving and retired – some of whom can go back to the years before World War 1'. Not much has happened either before or since then ... until now.

Almost all of the published reminiscences of police in this country during the past 150 years have been autobiographical. More significantly, they have been the tomes of noted retired policemen, including Alexander Tolmer (1882), Francis Augustus Hare (1892) and John Sadleir (1913); the antiquarian accounts of William Burrows (1859), A. L. Heydon (1911) and E. Morrow (1937); the largely unheralded (mostly unpublished) works of Thomas O'Callaghan earlier this century; and the adventures of the wonderful Detective Inspector Christie, first 'related' by J. B. Castieau in 1913 and unearthed again in 1993 by John Lahey in *The Public Life of Australia's Sherlock Holmes*. There have been several other less noteworthy works, with the principal exception to gender and antiquarianism, being the personal reminiscences of retired Victorian policewoman Elaine Brown, published in 1986. All these published works are distinguished by the senior police rank of their authors, the daring escapades of their subjects or the autobiographical ambitions of those who saw them into print.

The only recently published police-related works have been scholarly, historical or of the humorous genre, such as those written by Kerry Cue and Shirley Hardy-Rix. The dearth of published material by and about Australian coppers is due largely to the fact that policing in this country is a closed shop. We coppers rival staunch trade unionists for our solidarity, support of each other and our families and almost total exclusion of those who are 'not family'. We have also never been very good at baring our hearts and souls, and sharing our stories with others. A great paradox of policing is that much of our working lives is filled with pathos, daily drama and excitement – a world of action and intrigue that has captured the imagination of authors, script writers and the public for years but which, on a very personal – and human – level, we have been most reluctant to share outside the extended police family.

Then, at the end of the twentieth century, comes along the enigmatic Barry Dickins – not even an old copper; indeed, never a copper. And for those familiar with his writings of past years, more than likely a rogue, albeit literate and humorous.

Barry is an old Reservoir boy with the guile and worldliness of the streets. Without the use of warrant, summons, gun or battering ram he has penetrated, with his insight and pen, the hitherto closed world of the contemporary Australian police family.

The brotherhood syndrome, uniforms with para-military trimmings and innate police conservatism across the decades have perpetuated a stoic police façade of prosaic sameness: a world of 'Mr Plods'. Few authors, journalists, researchers or members of the general public have managed to breach this façade and touch the human faces behind it. The popular perception of police in this country is the imagery produced by cinematographic poseurs. This has not necessarily been a bad thing, because the relative insularity of the police family has engendered mutual trust, security and a very special camaraderie.

In this work Barry Dickins has sensitively reached beyond the mask of police homogeneity and found something of the rich tapestry of diversity, individualism, emotion, achievement and the at-times engrossing milieu of ordinary police lives. The individual stories are many and varied. They include the lot of Fred Silvester, former London 'bobby' and retired Assistant Commissioner, who during his heyday was feared and revered by Melbourne's underworld and known universally by his sobriquet 'The Cat'. He was a member of the cadre of incorruptible police, headed by the doyen of Australian policing, S.I. 'Mick' Miller, which as a group was once known as Australia's untouchables. However, in this work Fred reflects fondly on quieter and calmer times as a young bobby in London and a 'typical' country copper in Australia.

There is the O'Loughlin Dynasty: arguably Australia's best-known and successful police family, whose presence highlights the unique nature of kith and kin in 'the job', where it is commonplace for all those who are born into police families to be imbued with its ethos across generations.

The quiet Michael Reeves is a reminder of times changed. He managed to combine the dual careers of policeman and elite athlete, as an Australian rules footballer, and has been successful at both, yet today the demands of modern policing would preclude him from elite, professional sport. There was a time when many a policeman played league football, then went to work on a Saturday night, doing the rounds of fighting drunks in pubs.

And there are the women: Anne Wregg, Colleen Woolley, Jean Koch and Leeanne Holmes, who serve to remind us that the once all-male bastion of policing is no more. Women did not enter the police ranks in Victoria until 1917 and, dubbed 'police agents', it was not really until 1978 that they formally gained equal status with their male colleagues. In that context the work and exploits of Anne Wregg were both exciting and pioneering. The stories of these women are also a timely reminder that the police family extends beyond the uniform and embraces all those whose lives are daily (in some cases, irrevocably) touched by the dangers, pressures, shift-work and all-consuming nature of 'the job'. Here, too, is evidence of the enduring camaraderie extant in policing.

In retirement Colleen has been the chronicler of a published history of women police in Victoria and now works as volunteer secretary and newsletter editor for the Retired Police Association, which links hundreds of retired police across Australia, maintaining that immutable bond forged in the workplace.

Leeanne speaks warmly of the work of Police Legacy: an agency managed and funded by serving police, in a volunteer capacity, in support of hundreds of police widows and the children of deceased police women and men.

Michael Pratt, holder of the George Cross for bravery, who survived being shot in the back at close range by a criminal coward during a failed bank robbery, is a stark reminder that, on average since 1853, one member of the Victoria Police has been murdered every five years and hundreds of others have been accidentally killed, wounded or seriously injured.

Within these pages one will find the rich experiences of police – serving and retired, male and female – and the unique accounts of non-police members of 'our family', who married 'the job' and suffered grief and personal loss as their share of the 'copper's lot'.

This is not an academic treatise or the regurgitation of dates, facts and figures. Neither is it the lionisation of the unworthy, a tale of famous crimes or the dross of the hand-held camera hot on the trail of police machismo. These are the true stories of real people, told without embellishment. And importantly, they are the accounts of ordinary police, not chosen by rank, special favour or the self-selection of autobiography but because they have stories worth telling. Stories that are typical of thousands of police who have gone before – and indeed who are still serving and who have never before had a Barry Dickens to listen, and to articulate the feelings and words that have for so long been concealed in the heart and the soul.

This work gives voice to the spirit of more than 150 years of policing. Not a read for the tale of the fast car chase or the feel of television police action drama, this is a work of introspection. Read these words, empathise and understand, and share in the knowledge that never before has so much been told by those on the 'inside' of policing to an 'outsider'.

Barry Dickins has broken the code of silence and, in his own words, written 'something worthwhile and lasting ... a proper book'. And for that we are all the richer.

Robert Haldane, APM, PhD, BA (Hons)
Superintendent of Police

Contents

Introduction

Whom to thank for life? Our mothers or some higher benefactor? God, quite possibly, or the police if God doesn't fit. Although I am a practising agnostic and believe really that the voice of the people is the voice of God, all my life I have earnestly believed that we are placed on Earth to look after each other, even those in whom we can find nothing lovely.

When I reflect back over the fifty years I've been a child, a teenager, a vagrant and then a married father with an angelic little son who redeems me daily with the crust of love I find in his gorgeous eyes, I think I have no reason to thank the police at all. I thank my luck I met my wife, and that's it.

The police have, in the time I've been in the streets, never missed a chance to insult me or intimidate me. They haven't lifted a finger to help me, so why should I help them? Being a poet has few rewards apart from truthfulness and spirituality; and I never, in my wildest dreams, assumed I'd want to thank coppers. Perhaps coppers are the antithesis of writers? But one changes as one gets older ...

Being one who has long been interviewed *by* the police, the delicious irony doesn't escape me that it has felt like justice that I have interviewed *them* for a change.

Above all else this book is stories. It is tears, often, and some riotous laughter, had out the yakkety back in lonely police stations at ungodly hours, when yarning coppers have made me laugh until I've just about wept. Wept with the pity of it all. Wept out of shame for what the ungrateful community has put them through; as they are the first to admit, they are social workers as well as everything else.

People meet me in the street and say, 'What's the latest book?' I tell them it is interviews with police, and they invariably laugh and shriek 'Why bother with them?'

But protection keeps honest citizens from the Barbarians. Drugs are destroying our old innocence. I don't need my boy to grow up in a fragmented or disintegrating sub-society. I need my son to feel poised, not paranoid. I want cops around, and expect them to be around, for him as well as us, his mother and father. All mothers, all fathers. From the New Testament we read, when we've got the chance: 'No greater love hath a man than this: That he would lay down his life for his friends.'

Since many coppers I interviewed are practising Christians, some Catholics, lapsed or otherwise, or practising agnostics like myself, at the heart of these interviews is a search for faith and Greater Love. A greater meaning of Love. Sacrifice, you'd have to say. And the cops who went on the record here have given their lives without stint, to the often unthankful community, the ignorant community, and to their fellow cops in the Force. This book is a wake-up call for cops as well as citizens.

Duty and unselfishness are at the heart of the stories. Young policemen confronting oblivion, having to front a dying deposition, being shown snapshots by fellow officers to positively identify a lethal bank robber. Courageous policewomen who've ventured into neglected houses that make a slum look good. There they have discovered the faith to continue policing among the putrescent histories of abandoned kiddies. There they have helped. There they have loved us. With hands, feet, all the body, to save indifferent us. They've used heart and soul.

Someone said once 'The best lack all conviction, and the worst are filled with passionate intensity.' Well, that applies to modest police officers talking here of their gratitude to the Force, gratitude to fellow officers, gratitude to fortune itself for allowing them to carry on. Just as infantrymen during World War I fronted the horrors and drank up the madness of front-line trench warfare, so have Australian cops walked through flame to help the oblivious community.

I've learnt what occasional thanks means to police. A great many of them really feel unthanked. I suppose most of us do. A personal letter from a thankful parent means the slog is not for nothing. I'm writing that letter of thanks.

This, more than anything else, is a new book about a group we mostly take for granted. 'The Coppers will always be there for us' is what many people say, rightly or wrongly. The fact of the matter is that police are desperate for funds to fight crime, they are more than concerned about change, that a privatised Force wouldn't go in for the public as they've done over the years, over a century.

This is a book about police feelings. There are enough publications devoted to statistics and percentage points. In my opinion the time seemed right to listen to police as never before, to get the wax out and give the officers a chance to speak and let feelings tumble out. If they were very nearly killed, how did life feel when it was offered?

I've listened to police widows speak of the shock of losing a husband. The longing their memories provide these women with is inestimable. The loneliness and the daily grind fronting daylight on your Pat Malone. I have supposed the public may like to read of these women's earlier lives, know how it feels to forfeit the dearest friend you ever had: your loving husband.

These are not clichés, but the collected words to tell the tale of duty, determination, courage and single-mindedness, unselfishness often at the expense of everything. A crook back, recurring nightmares, death – physical as well as spiritual agonies due to the work. And what's the work? To ease the pain of living. Ease the pain of terror when it arrives in ghoulish forms as real as rapists or actual murderers.

Police work – who'd take it on? Who's brave enough? Plenty have been brave and gallant enough, not just giving it a tryout, but making a life of it, finding in the Force colleagues enough to last that lifetime.

I've listened to and spoken with veteran policemen who've remembered everything, and been glad to share their feelings, with time enough for a chance to set them down. Old men in little flats with rare tales of long ago, honest officers full of courage and rheumatism in equal measure. Rememberers of Squizzy Taylor, not that he ought to be remembered. Officers acquainted with rough brothels in downtown Fitzroy sixty-five years back, who've dived deep in the drain to fetch a few crims in for questioning all these years on. Policewomen who've protected raped girls awaiting trials of young offenders who've had their way with innocent kids. Policewomen who've defused psychotic bomb hoaxes and put up with extortionists at airport coffee lounges all in the line of duty. How did that feel? They have opened up their histories like flowers.

'Why interview police?' I am asked.

I reply: 'Why interview anyone?' Isn't there good in everyone?

Perhaps we should know our tribe. Know who arrests us, looks after us, keeps the law. 'What is law without order?' I ask of my detractors. What is society without hope?

Collected here are real stories of actual devoted policemen and policewomen who have more than contributed to our peace. They made it day in, day out. They intend peace. They have been slain, mocked, and caricatured. Not all police are exactly saints, of course. Several have been crooked and a fair few have been beyond the pale. But who are they really? Why did they join? Was not the original impulse to help us?

They did it for a job, that's obvious enough, but over the years the best police did it out of duty, duty to serve and protect children, adults, all of our tribe. Whatever we are, we need them badly – they served us and went in for us and went to Hell and back again in an effort to keep us safe from all harm. Ought we not to thank them?

At the heart of police feelings lies the truth. You have to venture to the feelings. They have been exhausted and over-whelmed by life's bizarreness, even though the pursuit of the desperate by the bizarre has often attracted them to their line of work or duty in the first place. Here police speak of memories and childhoods as openly as they talk about sieges, bloodletting, desperate ambulance journeys and the pity and wretchedness of seeing what drugs do to our kids.

I have looked for meaning and found hope in the recollections, responses and tragedies. The police speaking here aren't without a sense of humour, not above cracking a mordant joke or three if it suits their purpose. They say their humour in the Force is necessarily black to overcome the nature of the horror. It is a good black humour to be sure: you'd need it to put up with real horror stories breathed by historians themselves. After all, they have done it, they have fought and struggled with evil.

And evil isn't in any movie, by the way. It's tangible and confident. It stalks us in our streets doggedly. We turn on each other more and more. Who is unafraid? Who is without physical or interior apprehension? But toughness, even guts, is not enough. There has to be a guiding philosophy. For our families to be safe, for our minds and property to be safe, also, the public requires a Force to be reckoned with. Going by the souls interviewed over a year in back rooms of local police stations, and quiet muster-rooms and retired coppers' beach homes, we have one, no doubt of it. This book is a tribute to the Victoria Police Force. We shall only know how precious it is if it's gone. Heaven Forbid.

Above: Geoff O'Loughlin
with his mother
Geoff O'Loughlin
Joined Victoria Police 1968
Currently superintendent

Right:
Michael Reeves
Joined Victorian Police 1976
Resigned as sergeant 1989
Re-joined 1990
Currently senior sergeant

Front seat at the Greatest Show on Earth

Michael Reeves & Geoff O'Loughlin

One day I am sitting having a cup of tea with an old friend, Alan Lockwood, who's a raconteur, and he asks me what new book I'm up to. I pour him a splash of tea and say, 'I've just signed a contract to do a book about coppers – their lives – as a matter of fact.'

'What would you know about fact?' he says, 'Look at you.' And we laugh. Just like old friends laugh when they hit on the truth. But what is the truth? That's the question.

'How are you finding the police?' says Alan, nimbly dropping a cube of sugar into his tea. 'Wouldn't *they* be looking for *you*?' And we laugh again. I've always enjoyed Alan Lockwood's company. 'Are you interviewing only retired police? Or will some of them be active, Dickins?' I hadn't really thought about that. I was just thinking I'd try to find good storytellers who'd enjoy sharing their histories with readers.

'I know Geoff O'Loughlin, he's an old mate of mine. I met him at Apex,' says Alan, squinting at me and putting his neck on a tilt as if to say Why don't you talk to him? 'He's a Superintendent up at Broadmeadows Police Headquarters. He's pretty wild and you could say hot-headed. But brother, does he know how to spin a tale! Like a lot of Irish Catholics, he's all heart and all soul. He's not without a sense of humour and he's completely fearless. I'll give him a tingle for you, if you like. Got to go, mate. Work calls.' And he picks up his mobile and vanishes up the street.

I used to be slightly apprehensive, understandably, venturing into a police station, but not any more. The police are on the record and I am also. We're just talking, that's all. Just talking about duty, a calling, making a difference, childhood, horror stories, the whimsical, the here and now, and what it's like really to be a policeman.

I haven't got much reason to write a book of tributes to, or praise of, the police, when I think about how often I've been personally insulted, mocked, slandered, and temporarily incarcerated. But at the age of fifty, having been round the clock a few times, and having a little son not yet five, and violence being everywhere around, and life being so unpredictable and genuinely frightening, I'm starting to think about things like protection, and law and order, a lot more often lately. I want to put together a book about police feelings, leave the statistics to the scholars and the academics. What I'm good at is having people trust me and open up to me as if I am a gentle confessor. In fact, the interviews are a work of friendship.

Yesterday at Kangaroo Flat, just outside Bendigo, a deranged man shot four policemen during a siege. Victoria has always been violent. Fortunately, none of these officers died, but I wondered what they would have to say about police shootings. Them doing the firing. Us, the community that they strive to protect, also doing it. You'd have to say that shooting is booming. It's all the go.

Here's Broadmeadows Police Headquarters now – bleak, not exactly Frank Lloyd Wright. My eyes adjust like a camera lens to where I am. It's early on a Sunday morning and Michael Reeves will also be in the interview, which cheers me up, because he's a great footballer – not long ago one of Fitzroy's best men. And I've often cheered him on in the slosh. He's a man of guts and a practising Christian. So I have to say I haven't a nerve in me to go into this interview with these two men. I need coffee.

I'm in reception at the moment, in the utter quiet with a dull floor and the claustraphobic ceiling. It seems too early for crime or talk of it. I've been here ten minutes or so. It's only eight o'clock in the morning and there's not a foot squeal. Where are they?

Michael Reeves comes out of nowhere, the elegant athlete himself. Tall with an easy smile. 'Hello, mate,' he says. 'Come in and we'll try and find Geoff.' And I'm taken into a back room. What do I see here? Well, I can see the Whelan electric boiling water unit. It burbles away next door to its mates, the white humble plastic coffee or tea spoons. What's that? Kimsoft Kleenex are the

Broadmeadows Police sole luxury. There's the Police Credit Co-op brochure dispenser. A giant-size Black and Gold Table Salt container. An old Hitatchi TV in the corner, switched off.

Senior sergeant Michael Reeves folds his gum tree forearms across themselves. And he talks casually about growing up in Greensborough.

I ask him if he can remember saluting the flag when he was a boy because I'm looking for the patriotism, and the early idealism you need to go into the Force to make a difference, and help the community.

What, saluting the flag? Yeah, that's a vivid recollection for me. I went to St Mary's in Greensborough. You know, I had five brothers and sisters. We all went there. You know, in that time – the early '60s – everybody in the neighbourhood was sort of known to each other. In those years, it was a very white Anglo-Saxon sort of society. We all had bigger families – we were six kids, and all our neighbours were the same.

He laughs for some reason, at some internal comedy, then refolds his huge arms. I get the feeling he'd like to be out on the road again, instead of stuck inside doing office duties, answering the phone and so on.

'Was it tough in Greensborough, where you grew up, Michael?'

Oh, pretty tough. A game of war might turn into a stick fight, or stone throwing, but the next day you'd all be back. You know, mates. And life went on.

Suddenly he leaps up like a coil – there's this enormous coil. And he asks me sweetly if I want more black coffee. I always want more. 'Yes, please.'

There was a hopefulness in our neighbourhood. And honestly there were lots of good kids everywhere, there really were. It's the good ones you concentrate on. You had fights from time to time and you fought for justice.

'Was it love your neighbour or loathe your neighbour back then?'

Well, it had to be love your neighbour. Yes, that was the epithet. Most of those parents in that neighbourhood in Greensborough, the honest hard-working people who sincerely raised their kids the best way they knew how, we all keep in touch. And in our case there's always a barbecue or something in the summertime, or a picnic of some sort. You do try and keep in touch.

'What about your parents?'

My Dad got killed in a car accident when I was eleven and that changed all our circumstances. I got sent to boarding school after that. Up to Assumption College in Kilmore. The rest of the family stayed together. I was the oldest boy.

'The death of your father must have come as a real shock.'

He puts his hands across the sides of his face and the voice is lowered but he always looks me right in the eye. He sits on the edge of this desk and never really moves for the next few hours, going back over his life.

Oh, you know, I just couldn't believe it. My Dad was my hero. He played footy at North Melbourne and I think I was the only kid in the grade who had a dad who was a league footballer. He played for North and he played for Victoria. He played back pocket. Ruckman. He was John Reeves.

He cheers up with a sweeter memory out of nowhere.

When I was about nine I was picked as a boundary umpire with the Greensborough Blacks – didn't get a whistle – and I ran all the way home to tell my Mum about it. I can also remember the first time I was ever on the team sheet. You know, they'd stick up the team sheet at footy training and I was on it. So excited I was. I kept thinking, Jesus, I'm a boundary umpire – where do you go from here?

'Who were your footy heroes, Michael?' He lights up like a lamp. Bing!

Oh, Sam Kekovitch. This is in '69. Sam Kekovitch, at eighteen years of age he won the best and fairest at North Melbourne by sixty-seven votes. He was a real dynamo, Sam. And North had been a bottom-of-the-ladder side, just about since I was born, sort of thing. And I had never seen them successful, and then all of a sudden they had this player who could dominate the competition at eighteen years of age. He was just fantastic.

There are sounds now, suddenly. Sounds. As if a door is being opened somewhere and I can hear background muttering voices. It must be other coppers turning up for work. Gruff syllables turning up for work. I'm starting to wonder where Geoff O'Loughlin is. 'Let's try and find him,' says Michael, wondering, too.

I'm led into another room where Geoff O'Loughlin is speaking on the telephone at a desk covered with work. He has the unmistakable tough Irish Catholic look: thick set, with greyish-brown hair, chiselled. Hard-looking and gentle. Full of spark. I like him immediately, without knowledge. I think that's how it is in life: you either like people immediately and know them immediately or you are indifferent to them. He stands up to address me.

GO'L: What's this all about, mate? This interview. It's not for a newspaper, is it?

'No, it's a book, Geoff. Something worthwhile and lasting. A book of police experiences and feelings. It's not for the press. It's a proper book.'

GO'L: What do you want to talk about?
MR: We've been talking about footy.

GO'L: Well, I don't know whether this is worth printing or not, but my first recollection of a constable was with my late brother Barry, who was a vehement Collingwood supporter. And there was this other policeman, Fred. Now Fred's gone, unfortunately – they're both gone. But they were rough, tough, consorting squad detectives. I was ten years of age, standing in the outer at Victoria Park, and all of a sudden this long-haired peanut jumps up and throws a full can of beer at the mounted police doing the boundary patrol. He misses the policeman and hits the horse on the rump. Everybody saw it, and this kid ducks down in front of us. I'm looking at my brother, thinking, 'He's a policeman and justice will prevail, they'll do something about him.' They did: they hit him. And I thought, 'That's how you be a policeman. You hit him.' And everyone in the crowd – about fifty people immediately around him – seen them do it. They've all just nodded their head and I thought, 'Oh, yeah, that's justice. C'mon Collingwood!' And I can remember that to this day: he was just up there against the cyclone fence, knocked out. They didn't want to miss their team playing. Different action for different times. Forty-two years ago.

For a moment there is nothing to say. We are in the past, all right. I can hear it hum. Both officers are like sentinels. You can see the ease between them. It's obvious they are best friends. Geoff's fifty-two. Michael's just turned forty, but his face looks considerably older. He's a veteran acquainted with horror but he has this boyish, sweet nature that overwhelms anything gruesome. He's sunny. That's all. Loves life.

GO'L: I can remember being so proud of my two older brothers in the police. When I was young they meant so much to me. I idolised them. The way they learned their evidence walking up and down the house – because you couldn't refer to your notes at that time – pages of evidence for a drunk driver. And I can remember feeling so proud of these people ... You know, 'My brothers are looking after the community.'

We'd lived in Northcote all our life until I was seventeen, and then we moved to Watsonia. But I can recall my brother used to police the Northcote High School pupils and they used to tell me these stories of what happened to them on Saturday night at the police station. And I used to go home and challenge my brothers. And they'd say, 'Who said that?' And I'd say so-and-so, and they'd say, 'Look, that kid did a burglary. He's a sniffling little sook. And he's done this and done that.' And once, one of my brothers came down and challenged one of these kids, to prove to me that what he was saying was a pack of lies.

I was a big-time Sharpy when I was a kid, between seventeen and nineteen, when the Sharpies were in. I went through a phase when I resented the police.

And then my brother – two other brothers – were cadets. Out of the five brothers, I was the only one who wasn't in the police force. And at that stage, I'd gone from idolising the Force and the justice they were doing to being anti-Them; I was swayed by peer group pressure, because some of my mates were bloody dills. And my late brother Barry tried to talk me into joining the job, and I said, 'Why would I want to join the job, the way you treat the people?'

I said to myself, 'Yes, I want to be a policeman, and I'll show my brothers the type of policemen they should be.' And years later, I turned out to be exactly like them, because there was nothing wrong with them anyway. They were perfect models anyway.

And he said, 'All right. You join the police force, and you can be the type of policeman you want to be. If you want to let someone go, you can. You can make the decision whether you lock that person up or not.' And I remember that was the moment when I said to myself, 'Yes, I want to be a policeman, and I'll show my brothers the type of policemen they should be.' And years later, I turned out to be exactly like them, because there was nothing wrong with them anyway. They were perfect models anyway. But I remember thinking at the time, I'll get in and I'll be a different sort of policeman. I'll be the social worker policeman.

They tell of how they met.

GO'L: At the Greensborough Police Station, that's where we met. I was a detective and Michael was a cadet.

MR: I was a cadet there and Geoff was a senior detective, at the time. And I remember on my last day as a cadet, when I was seventeen, they took me down the pub, giving me advice. (*He turns to Geoff.*) And I remember going home and writing down some of the things you said to me. I remember you saying 'Be firm, but always be fair', and writing those things down, and saying to myself, 'Right, this is what I'm going to be.'

GO'L: I'm ten years older than Michael and we've been best friends ever since.

MR: Yeah. And I can remember Brendan Cole and others – obviously detectives. These blokes have been involved in sieges, you know, investigating armed robberies and stuff. And I thought, 'They're your heroes.'

GO'L: The more senior members, some are dills, but some of them have so much charisma you do hold them in a sort of reverence. And you learn very early: look at the good points of your sergeants and copy them, and ignore the others. So out of six sergeants that you're working with, you'll become the better policeman.

'So, it's trial and error. You're looking for the perfect example.'

We're a group of people that will go anywhere, anytime, for anyone. There aren't too many organisations that will do that.

GO'L: I worked with Carl Stillman for eighteen months. He was the most tenacious thief-catcher you would ever get. He just had a sixth sense for crooks. He had this ability – he would pull up twenty, thirty cars a night, and people would say, 'Jeez, you're lucky.' But it's not luck, it's volume. He used to say, 'They don't walk around with a stamp on their head, Geoff.' This was very good advice. You've got to wade through ninety-six per cent of decent people to get to the shit. I can't remember whether it was Carl who said this, or if it was something that I just believe in myself. If it wasn't Carl, he certainly inspired that feeling. But you've got to be careful you don't treat that ninety-six per cent poorly. That's one of the problems our young police have. They typecast.

You've got to get to that four per cent of the community – it might be ten per cent now because of the drugs. Look, we're a group of people that will go anywhere, anytime, for anyone. There aren't too many organisations that will do that.

You speak of idealism. Well, let me tell you about my father, who I loved dearly, and who was so proud of having five sons in the police force. God, he was so righteous, so thorough and such a decent man. My parents were the greatest thing going. Mum gave us kindness and Dad gave us integrity and strength to do the right thing all the time. My father, he always said, 'You've got to be ten per cent better than everybody else if you're going to be a policeman. That's what I've told your brothers. That's what I'm telling you.' I can hear him saying it now.

'How were arguments settled around the O'Loughlin table in the old days?'

GO'L: Well, he'd start an argument. He'd start one up. He'd be there waiting for us. He was retired, waiting for us to come for tea and he would say something that was right out of left field and we would all argue with him. He loved it. And we are all still doing it to this day. We still argue every time we're together. It's almost a tradition. At the '99 Grand Final, Ben's arguing with Neil – the constable's arguing with the deputy commissioner about something to do with the police force. We're a family that loves involvement and passion – and Dad loved nothing more. He brought us up the right way.

He slowly stands up straight and stretches his arms out, relaxing. These blokes haven't moved in all this time. The phones haven't begun ringing. It's still early. I can hear a few doors banging downstairs at reception. First citizens coming in to talk to police about this or that. I can hear a laugh and some scuffed footsteps.

GO'L: When we were younger, and there were so many of us at the table, to settle these disputes, Mum would pick up the high-tin loaf of bread and throw it at the person who was making too much noise. That was the signal – because there were *fourteen* people at our table! – that was a signal to give it a rest. And you did as she said. She was Law. Mum used to say, 'If you can't say something nice, don't say anything at all.' I've used Mum's philosophy in my life – 'If I wished one attribute on the whole of society, it'd be kindness' because that would fix most problems in society.

> *I've got myself into all sorts of trouble, sticking my neck out, trying to help people. But that's what you're there for.*

Mum would always make us stick up for the underdog. Always. There was a kid at Helen Street State School. His parents were in

19

concentration camps, and when you touched him, he screamed. Because of Mum's philosophy, making me look after the less fortunate, I would end up sticking up for him, getting into trouble with the older kids. There was another kid called Perry Anderson, with an egg-shaped head, who used to get called 'egghead' and used to break down and cry. Because of Mum's upbringing, I used to go and defend these people. Luckily, I had older brothers – when I got into a fight with the older kids picking on the less fortunate, my brothers used to come and help out. Especially Barry. He had an awesome reputation. They were rough, tough days. But that's the way I was brought up. Michael will tell you, we're that type of people: we go and look after the underdog – and he does, too. The only time I've ever got in trouble in the police force is helping people – not myself. Once again Mum's influence.

MR: Let me tell you a story about drunks. We used to have hundreds at City West. I'm talking about every single shift. You'd do an afternoon shift and there'd be some nights where you locked up a dozen of them. Particularly cold nights, where they'd come out and put themselves in a position where they knew if they lay there the coppers'd come. Because they had to get out of the cold.

GO'L: It was sad, too.

MR: There was this old bloke Cyril, used to hang around the Victoria Markets all the time. And he was the dirtiest – you know, some of these blokes had lost control of their bowels and everything. It was not pretty.

'I suppose it's degrading, seeing them in that state, is it?'

MR: Yeah, it was. You used to have to do it, though, as a young constable, and you had to search them. That was part of it.

GO'L: It was dangerous too, doing that sort of work. You'd put your hand in and they'd often have a razor blade on them.

MR: Or a turd. You know, it was unbelievable, the things that'd happen to you. They'd have a spew all over you. You're picking them up without any protection, you know. We didn't have personal protection kits or special gloves like we've got now.

GO'L: We used to have to hose the van down at the end of the shift. You felt sorry for them. And that was your job. What else could you do? If you didn't give them a sleep they were in a lot of trouble.

'Well you have the patience now, in middle age. You know, you've been through life, haven't you? You two blokes have seen everything. You've seen things the public wouldn't credit.'

MR: I think you're right about patience. I think in those days blokes like that were an inconvenience, that's all. When you're an eighteen or nineteen or twenty-year-old young constable, looking for criminals, these sort of blokes are just in the way and taking up all your time.

Michael moves. The first time in ages. Stands up and stretches his arms and yawns, then cracks his finger knuckles and drums them on the table.

MR: I have an affection and a revulsion for drunks. It was drink as opposed to drugs when I started out twenty years ago. You'd lock up a dozen drunks. Lanes all over North Melbourne. It seemed a thousand or a hundred of them used to be there.

I assume this means lifting them up to see if they're animate.

GO'L: When I first joined the job in 1968 we had our own 'resident' drunk at Kew – each station had one – and his name was Stanley Mollison, we gave him a birthday cake when we locked him up for the hundredth time. Someone had gone through the book and said, 'This is your hundredth conviction', so they bought a cake. And we all sang, 'Happy Birthday' to him, and he started crying. He was one of Australia's top violinists, who lived in Kew, and his wife left him for another person. Once that happened he went downhill and was on the metho.

But he was a lovely, lovely man who used to go and cry outside his wife's house, and she'd ring up and say, 'Stanley's here.' And, 'Come on, Stanley.' 'Oh, hello, Geoffrey.' You got to know him. And when we trained the young constables, who were a bit rough with him, we'd say 'Don't talk to him like that. Leave him alone.' You realised that he had his dignity but got to the stage where he was drinking methylated spirits, but he was still scared of the metho. He'd have it in his coat, disguised in a Coca-Cola tin, and he'd have a sip then say *'whoo-whoaaa ...'* and shake his head. Eventually killed him, the old bugger.

'But you loved him. He was a part of everything, wasn't he?'

GO'L: He was a lovely old man, and you looked after him. And he would say to Mr Daniher, the local magistrate, I'm a hopeless old drunk.' 'No, you're not, Mr Mollison,' the magistrate would reply. Then: 'I apologise. It won't happen again, sir.' But it always did. You know, there was nowhere to put these people except gaol.

MR: I see them come through the cells now, the ones that I used to lock up at West Heidelberg and Preston, and you get to know them after a time. Although you're never mates with them, there is that relationship – 'I knew you fifteen years ago' – and they're really glad to see you when they come into the police station, pleased that you remember their name.

This seems to me the utopian aspect of police work.

GO'L: Look, let's just talk about drugs for a second. Heroin. O.K.? Let's update everything. The way crime has changed because of the heroin epidemic, not just in Melbourne but all around Australia. But let's just talk about Melbourne now. People, some legitimate honest people, without any prior convictions, become junkies for various reasons and will then do anything to score. They will arm themselves and enter people's homes, seeking television sets or CDs. Anything at all to sell to get a score. And they become so reckless and so suddenly violent in their desperation to score heroin. They will king hit someone at an ATM machine, to get a few bucks. That never happened in the old days, right? Am I right?

These days, a large percentage of all our crime is drug oriented. These people are aggressive. Not just men – women, too. And they're young. This new aggression all over the place, it's difficult to deal with. We never had that problem when we were young policemen. It is much harder policing in today's environment. And this type of person doesn't give a shit about anybody. They just want their next hit.

'Who's the most unfortunate person you've ever had to help? Does one person in particular stand out from all the others? Where you almost forgot that you were a policeman, where you've really helped someone, forgetting what your actual job is, and probably taking more time with it than you should?'

MR: You often feel frustration that you can't do enough for people. The memory that comes to me is sitting in the police car at West Heidelberg Police Station. I'd been out on patrol and was about to come back and go inside when a little face appeared at the window. And this little voice says, 'My name's Toby. I'm six.' And I said, 'Hello, Toby. My name's Michael Reeves and I'm twenty-three.' And I said to him, 'What can I do for you, Toby?'

And he said, 'My Mum and Dad take drugs, and my Mum puts a thing on her arm, and ...' He went through the whole thing, and told me he had a sister, Amber. Then at the end of it he said, 'I want to get a new home.' And he's six years old.

I'll never forget it. Young Toby would now be twenty or something now, you know.

GO'L: I wonder where he is.

MR: So anyway, I went round to the house where Mum and Dad were living and when I pulled back the kids' bed coverings, I remember they were black. The sheets were black and wet and putrid, you know. There was used syringes lying about the house. Pornographic stick books – and I'm talking about real porno stuff; magazines, lying out on the couch; and these little kids. Just dirt and filth and everything, and these two were living in all of that. Mum and Dad would shoot up in front of these kids, and I just couldn't believe it.

GO'L: I've heard that story twenty times and can never get used to it!

Geoff's face is florid. Neither exasperated nor relieved, full to the brim with social justice as he'd practice it personally. He's thinking about what he can do, and what he's done in over thirty years of putting himself through all sorts of things for the Victorian community. He seems to look down at his brawny arms for the stories and find them there. He only looks up at me when he's collared one. It is then that he speaks. You can tell that these men are old friends because they never interrupt one another.

GO'L: Michael is an excellent policeman and he goes beyond what is expected – never boasts! Listen. Michael's raised over sixty thousand dollars for Somalis in his area. He's been their mentor. He's been absolutely marvellous. He is what policing at the turn of the century is all about: looking after the community and getting involved.

Michael doesn't know where to look, being shy and unassuming. He just gives an awkward sort of smile.

> *If there's not somebody else to do it, it's our job. That's basically what policing is. If there's not somebody else to take charge of it, it's our job, along with the other things we're nominated to take charge of.*

'Geoff, the long list of instances of police looking after people, is that list endless?'

GO'L: What do you reckon, Michael? Never-ending!

MR: If there's not somebody else to do it, it's our job. That's basically what policing is. If there's not somebody else to take charge of it, it's our job, along with the other things we're nominated to take charge of, of course.

GO'L: As a twenty-something year old, you're a social worker. I can remember going to a house where the wife answered the door in the nude. I'm only twenty-two, something like that. She's got her dressing-gown on, but it's open. The first thing I see is this nude woman in front of me. I say, 'Are you right?' She says, 'Oh, sorry, sorry, sorry.' And she sits me down and she says, 'You've got to talk to my husband. He keeps, ah, it's not rape,' she says, 'but he likes to think it is. He comes in and he throws me on the bed, and he rips all the clothes off me, and he does it to me.' She says, 'I don't mind that, it doesn't hurt me or anything – but it costs me a fortune in clothes. Can you do something about it?' And, at twenty-two years old, just a boy, I'm going, 'Ahhh ...' (*Laughing*)

'How strange!'

GO'L: 'Oh, all right ...' And I went in to my mate for advice and said, 'The husband's rooting her, but he's ripping all her clothes when they're having sex.' He says, 'What? He's in the van.' And this colleague's young, too. So, we discuss it together and go in and we tell the husband that the best way around it is to tell her how you feel when you get the urge, and she'll put her old clothes on. I said, 'Now, is that all right?' He said 'Yes, thanks.'

The three of us roar laughing. I mean it is crazy.

'So when you go through the door of someone's home, is it rather like the Twilight Zone? Is that the appeal of police work? You know, the strangeness and the danger, is that why you go into it, or part of the reason at least?'

MR: Absolutely!

GO'L: You don't know what you're walking into. And that's how you like it – each day is different.

MR: I have twice – well, this was when I was working in Broadmeadows – I have twice walked in to one particular house and seen son having sex with Mum. He was fourteen. That's what people should realise. That we have to be able to handle any situation that arises.

There is one particular woman in West Heidelberg that I had to lock up. Remember, Geoff? She blew up a car in the street. She hated all her neighbours. She had a family full of people you could not believe. Her ten-year-old daughter got pregnant and got her head blown off by the father who was boarding at their place. Their home was just the most dysfunctional place. People you couldn't believe had a family, you know what I mean? So Mum set fire to three different houses in the same neighbourhood, just because she didn't like the neighbours. And one of them actually saw her do it, eventually, and I went and charged her. Prior to that, she also blew up the car of the bloke who lived opposite, using gelignite. You wouldn't think, would you, this is just a Mum living in the suburbs.

'She knew how to set off gelignite, did she?'

GO'L: She knew about gelignite, and she blew the car out of the street because he used to park across the driveway in a way that inconvenienced her.

'And that annoyed her, did it?'

GO'L: (*laughing*) That's right.

'I'm starting to like her.' We all laugh. Is this real life? Good as?

GO'L: You'd be no good on the jury.

MR: The day the neighbour told me he saw her throw that Molotov cocktail, I went into the house and Dad, who was a big fat guts, was lying on the couch. You know, watching the TV, lying out sideways watching the TV, and I've come in, and I've said, to her, 'You're under arrest, for arson. You're not obliged to say anything ...' I said all the proper things, you know. And she hit me with a beer bottle – because she's standing there, drinking, necking a beer bottle – bang. (*He laughs.*) And Dad didn't move off the couch. He's looking around trying to work it all out – what's this going on? And I've got the handcuffs on, dragging her through the place. He didn't even get off the couch. It was unbelievable. People don't realise what you have to put up with.

'When you joined up, Michael, did you realise how bizarre some of the cases would be?'

MR: No, you had no idea what it'd be like. You went into it for the excitement. I know that.

GO'L: I went into it for the same reason. You're full of idealism and you think everybody is just like you. You think everybody comes from the same upbringing, with the same values. But you just haven't got a clue what's going to come. Police say this is a front-row ticket to the Greatest Show on Earth.

And this is the whole frustration I keep talking about. The judges and the lawyers wouldn't have a clue, because they don't see it. They don't see the bloke that's tried to garrot himself in a cell, the prisoner that puts shit all over himself – 'bronzing up', as it's called – and says, 'I'm going to come round and fuck your mother', or threatened to bash you up. They see him the next day, sitting in his office, saying, 'The police picked on me! The police did this. The police did that. I wouldn't do such a thing.' The judge sees him on his best behaviour, and then they say, 'Well, why didn't you just go and reason with this man? He seems an intelligent person.' Police did try to reason with him in his raw state. The lawyers and judges don't see the raw state, not in the court.

'How do you deal with insane persons? People who are certifiably insane but still living at home.'

GO'L: Now, in many cases, the government has given these problem people halfway houses to live in because they have shut down institutions for some reason. I'll give you an example. This is how bad our society's gone. I'm driving down the road with my daughter – this is about five or six years ago – and here's a bloke masturbating on the corner of the street. I was going to get out and grab this fellow, and my daughter said, 'Oh, Dad, that so-and-so.' I said, 'You know about him?' She said, 'Yeah, he's a bit early, he does that normally till the school bus arrives.' This is my daughter, probably about twelve. I said, 'What are you talking about?'

It emerges that he's in the halfway house down the road, and one day he was out there playing with himself, and the girls yelled out at him and whistled. So now he puts a show on when the bus drives past. Right? Now, a lot of neighbours are saying, 'Well, what are the police doing about it?' Well they can't do anything, because he's a nut. He's in a halfway house and they tell him to stop, but they can't lock him up because our society has allowed him to leave one institution. He can't be reasoned with because of his condition. So we can't put him anywhere. It becomes acceptable behaviour in the '90s that would not have been allowed in the '70s. Who's right? So he just does it. Their hands are tied. Now, I don't know the full story, but that's an example of how society has changed.

That's why we had so much trouble in the '80s and some police used their guns, for example. One person had slashed himself about nineteen times. The police got called there and this person walked towards them. When we turned up there, they turned on us. The person walks towards the policewoman. She pulls her gun and says, 'Drop it, drop it, drop the knife!' And bang, she shoots the person in self-defence.

Know what the lawyers say? 'Why didn't you use your baton?' Why? He's mutilated himself nineteen bloody times – what's a belt over the head going to achieve, and you have to get close to the knife to do it? And they only have to be lucky once. They only have to slash us once and we're dead. Right? We've got to be lucky all the time. They only have to be lucky once. And with a knife.

He stops suddenly, changing tack.

What are you going to do with all these stories? We're baring our souls here. You know that, do you?

'Well that's what I wanted. To collect the feelings. Tell me something, Geoff. When you look at heroes, for example, or models on whom you've based your life, what sort of people are they?'

GO'L: If you're asking whether there are people in my life who've turned me around, very definitely. For me it was my brothers. I know I keep saying that. We used to all sleep in the bungalow together. My brother, Barry, he died in 1972. He used to say, 'Hit first, apologise later. You're a long time dead.' I had them all on a pedestal.

I remember we got a call at the station to go to Kew Cottages when I was twenty years old. (I was stationed at Kew in 1969.) There'd been an excavation hole dug in which was ten inches of boiling water. The hole was eight foot by three – that's a few metres by a metre. A ten-year-old kid, he'd got out of the home and fallen into this hole, which was like a well. There was a Yugoslav bloke who worked there and he hadn't locked the door because he couldn't read the English-language sign saying to keep the door shut at all times. (*His face looks resigned to everything that can happen. He sighs.*) The superintendent of the Cottages was sacked – couldn't do anything about it. So he called us police.

The body of this child had boiled in this drain, and we had the responsibility to get him out. I remember using two rakes, one each side, to try and lever him out. We were just as upset as everybody else but we, at twenty years of age, were expected to take charge. Every time we got the body level to the ground, back down he would fall. In desperation I decided to fill up the large hole with water from a nearby fire hydrant. Everybody just stood there watching two twenty year olds make decisions.

It took two hours for the hole to fill up. But the body didn't float because it was stuck in the mud. I looked at my mate Maurie Webb, hoping he would volunteer to dive down and get him, or I would have to. I was the senior man by three numbers (we were squad mates). While we were both trying to muster up some courage, the boy floated to the top. I was so relieved I grabbed him and placed him in the stretcher.

I had nightmares about that for three days. As I said, you never know what you are going to face when you go on duty. But you do it because you're the only one to do it. Isn't that right, Michael? Isn't that how it was when you started, when you were a rookie?

MR: That's right, Geoff. I had a horror experience. It would have been either '78 or '79 and I can still remember the address. I'd better not give it. Shots fired. How old am I? Twenty years. I went there with Steve Campbell, mate of mine. I was a young constable. We pulled up right in front of the house. He came out firing a fifteen-shot semi-auto at us and went back in. It was a siege. And we had the new .38s. And I'm thinking, 'I'll shoot this bloke if he comes out, right up to us, I'll shoot him.' All this happened within about a minute and a half of us getting there. We were on the three o'clock shift. This is 4.30 pm. I'll never forget all this thick coagulated blood coming out of his head after he shot himself, right in front of us. And the way I could hear his teeth clicking and saying, 'I hate coppers.' Right through that thick volcano of blood.

Geoff speaks in a hush.

GO'L: There are criminals, it's true, who are beyond redemption. The lowest form of life – people capable of horrendous things. We have to deal with them. Who else does? I had one that locked four kids in a toilet and poured petrol over them, threatened to kill them unless he got money.

> *It's far better now than it was in the early days – far more professional: there is help available. All we had was a drink with a mate or a talk with your wife or friend.*

It's the abandoned children who get to you most. And the police must deal with them. This perhaps eludes the ignorant public.

Let me tell you about what happened at Ambon Street, Preston. We went to this house where all the sheets were black and the carpets were, seriously, like an ashtray. I thought there was a mural on the wall; it was actually a meal that had been thrown there three months earlier. We have to help these kids. We're social workers as well as everything else.

It's far better now than it was in the early days – far more professional: there is help available. All we had was a drink with a mate or a talk with your wife or friend.

'Do you ever get sick? Ever have a day off? Ever get the flu? Are you ever not up to it, work I mean?'

GO'L: In our day you never went sick, especially on night shift, because you were letting your mates down.

Do you still get excited coming to work, Geoff, at fifty-two? You've been a copper thirty-two years. Are you sick of it?

GO'L: Look. I still get excited coming to work. Some of us don't. I'm lucky. Five years ago, I was having dinner with a mate of mine. And I was on night shift, and he said to me, 'What are you going at nine for?' I said, 'I want to get to work.' He said, 'You don't start till eleven.' I said, 'I just want to get there, and get prepared.' And he said, 'You still love your job, don't you?' He said, 'Oh, mate, I would love to have that feeling. I've made millions' – he's a panel beater – 'but I hate going to work.' And I said, 'Well, I'll never be rich, but I'll always have a wonderful job.' I enjoy it. And that's the choice I made. Well, that's about it, I think.

He wishes me luck with the book and heads off back to his work, saying 'Take him on a tour, Michael.'

Now Michael leads me to the holding cells and the first thing I see is a big panel full of black and white video screens that depict inmates and barrenness simultaneously. I look in there and think Poor buggers. There are two men, barefooted with crew cuts, plainly visible on the screen, just lying on the floor in white t-shirts. They look about thirty. An officer gets hold of a large bunch of keys, and unlocks doors for us to go in. There's a loud noise whenever a lock is undone with a key. Michael shows me a big white card stuck alongside the names of each prisoner on the video screen. This card tells you whether they're allergic to any foods, such as pork.

We have to be very careful what they eat. Some have allergies to different things, and you can't afford to upset them.

I go into the cells with Michael. Two long pale men are flaked out on thin mattresses with arms folded behind their heads. One of them is staring up at the concrete ceiling and the other must be just staring at his stomach, as he is inclined downwards. They look subdued, to say the least. Michael saunters past one of them and playfully pushes the edge of his sheet where his toes are and says, 'How're you going, knackers? You all right?' There's a soft grunt, by way of reply.

I am told police have to hold some prisoners at Broadmeadows for months, due to overcrowding in larger jails.

I drove home filled with a mixture of admiration and bafflement, wondering just how these cops keep it together. They're tough, very tough, and honest. And Christian. And both of them are brilliant rememberers. They are, in fact, active police historians. Unless they loved our community, with all of their heart and soul, I doubt they could do the police work. I believe they separate us from chaos and barbarianism. I'm glad they're here. I know that. And in my heart I thank them.

Michael Pratt
Joined Victoria Police 1973
Retired due to ill-health 1979
Returned as unsworn member 1996

It's very close, the police force

Michael Pratt

Recipient of the George Cross Award for Valour

The Broadmeadows Police Headquarters seem to have become a home away from home for me over the past couple of months. Here, among the hard slog of active police service, I have been witness to several moments of sweetness.

Today I am to meet Michael Pratt, the winner of the highest civilian award for valour: the George Cross. This he received for a deed he thought nothing of: a do-or-die struggle in 1976 with desperate bank robbers who were engaged in knocking off the Heidelberg Road, Clifton Hill, branch of the ANZ bank. It was an off-duty morning when Constable Pratt was motoring by with the intention of having a trim at an uncle's barber shop, George, almost next door.

He is fortunate to be living, because he was shot at point-blank range by one of the armed robbers, Norman Faure, in the upper region of his back. Not being armed at the time, Constable Pratt took direct action in the affray. He had into them with the only weapon he could scrounge from the boot of his vehicle – a jack handle.

In the course of a particularly violent engagement, Constable Pratt showed just what he was made of, and got shot for it. He is back at work at the moment, at Broadmeadows Police Headquarters, after enduring pain that might perhaps have been unendurable and permanent for anyone else. Twenty-four years of pain.

Michael Pratt greets me at reception and at first glance appears ominously quiet – neither friendly nor unfriendly. He escorts me into a plain-looking back room where we sit opposite each other. He grasps his palms and looks at me with perfect candour. His countenance betokens quickness of response, eagerness, and a vague suspicion, probably because police do all the questions, but now I'm to ask a few.

He is thickset, with whitish–grey, previously fair hair, and appears somewhat older than his forty-five years. He has just celebrated his birthday, in fact: the forty-fifth marvel of his life, given what's occurred to him. His eyes dart whenever he remembers the past but settle whenever we are back in the present. This is to begin with.

His childhood: what of it? He seems surprised when I ask him about his early days, but they come back. It's quite hard to tell whether he's enjoying the early part of his life in the telling, but there are a few short laughs along the way. He has the most inscrutable face.

He's not moving to begin with. Rock-still, intense.

Born in Macleod – well, really East Melbourne first: born at The Mercy. Five brothers and sisters: Peter, Susan, Mark, Daniel and Matthew. Our household? What was it like? Lively and raucous.

Ghost of a grin. Now it's gone.

My youngest brother, Matthew, is thirty, thirty-one or so. Dad was, well, my hero. He was a spare parts automotive worker – selling spare parts for a number of Ford outlets. Laboured in factories. He had what you'd call a photographic memory for spare parts manuals. Came in very handy. He was keen on the Carlton Football Club. The father of one of his friends was the caretaker of the club, so Dad could get in and see the game. I played a bit of footy for the Watsonia Football Club. Half-back or flank. This is from junior level to senior level.

He doesn't seem too keen on footy.

School? St Martin of Tours Catholic primary school. Then on to Christian Brothers in Alphington. I did Preston Tech. Fourth Year. Accounting-type study course. As a matter of fact, when I was eighteen I went for three different jobs. I wanted to be all three things: policeman, fireman, ambulance officer. I went to the local police station and sent in all the forms. I would've been happy to do any one of those jobs, but the police job came back first, so that was it.

'You were educated by the Brothers. Were they tough?'

Yes, the Brothers were tough. But it was necessary, that strictness. It was a recognition of authority.

'A spiritual biff behind the ear?' We move on ...

Large classrooms, Fifty-three or -four in the class. Old-style flip-top wooden desks. The teacher was right on top of you. You said 'Good morning, Brother.' He did the roll call. If you weren't present, the Brother would ring the parents to see what the situation was. We did such things as Morning Prayer. They were just average, my school days. Sort-of everyday. If there were any disputes, the Brothers usually sniffed them out. It's an instinct, sorting out disputes. They could see it in your face. Yes, that quality helped me later.

He leans to his left, then sits upright again. His tie is done up tight. Everything is.

School contributes to your sense of authority. My Mum says it's in the breeding. It's just the way Mum and Dad spoke in the house. They're your role models. The Christian Brothers' values inspire you, just like your parents' do.

He is neither relaxed nor tense, but somewhere in between.

My Dad worked three jobs. Apart from the auto game, he worked for the Melbourne City Council, cleaning offices; and he did tow truck work as well, at night, for Watsonia Cartage – a well-established business, been there many years. He'd be working behind the counter, selling spare parts, then the boss'd say 'There's a prang down the road.' Dad'd take the dustcoat off and away he'd go. (*His eyes enlarge, remembering that sense of family honour.*) He'd come home afterwards and be back in bed ten minutes, then off again.

I can't hear a single thing in this room except his voice. There's no whirring Coke machine or even a silent one. No birds outside and no other police voices save his.

As a young fellow I enjoyed reading movie books (you know, movie biographies), sports books – I liked the statistics – and I had an interest in the Stock Market ... stats and shares. If I'd gone on with the accounting, maybe I would have ended up having something to do with the Stock Exchange. (*But then he wonders what men are worth and rubs his considerable chin.*)

'What were the highlights and the lowlights of your childhood?'

When I was eighteen months old I had pneumonia. Mumps a little later on. No broken legs or arms. Had a left knee reconstruction when I was eighteen. Ours was a tight family. Close. Mum always had a cooked meal. No take-away in those days! When Dad got in late off the tow trucks he never had to scrounge something cold to get stuck into in the dark. Mum'd always have something hot waiting for him. He'd finish one o'clockish on a Saturday: she'd have it timed so he had it as he crossed the door. (*He becomes mobile for the first time, waving his arms to show this.*)

'Other memories?'

For kids growing up in Melbourne at that time it was always a treat when your Gran and mum took you to Coles and Myer's. You'd look up and stare at all the huge buildings. And think, How good is this? What a big place it is!

So like a child – eager and trusting.

As I said before, the set routine, the discipline – you get it all from home. Dad would never run anyone down. If he had anything negative to say about anyone, once was enough. There was no swearing. You might be allowed a few 'bloody's, but if you mentioned the *other* you were in deep poo! (*He shakes his hands together and they clasp hugely.*)

'What sort of tow truck did he drive?'

A big '52 Ford. Heavy Salvage with a crash box: those were the gearboxes you could change gear in, even if you did the clutch. You picked the right revs and crashed through. You could hear him coming alright. We'd be out playing on the street and you'd hear the roar.

His voice is the same but is becoming somehow soothed.

A few times when cars were bogged Dad went out and picked them out, got the winch up. Real bad accidents upset him, I know that much. He had a few people die in his arms.

He was never, ever scared of anyone and he never did wrong by anyone. My father practised 'Love thy neighbour' but he didn't let anyone do the wrong thing by him, either. Dad was quiet inside. But you wouldn't want to cross him. Dad wasn't a great talker. He was more a doer!

Are you like him? I wondered.

Dad sometimes scrounged not-genuine parts for people who had pranged cars, rather than have them pay top dollar to a wrecker. If he saw a bike frame down at the tip, he'd take it home and do it up. Straighten the spokes. He used to say 'Everything will come in handy one day – everything will be useful.'

He was a natural leader, in a way, Dad. 'Coz he treated everyone the same, basically. It was in his approach. It's all in the approach. Tow truck operators have always had a pretty bad name – they have traditionally been known as vultures – but Dad wasn't one of those. When he spoke to people who'd been smashed up in a crash he always said 'Are you all right?' If it was a bad accident, he'd be pretty shook up after it. When he came home, Mum'd get up and have a de-brief with him, and they'd sort it out over the family tea table till he was right to go to bed – briefly.

> *As a teenager you either heard the call or you didn't. My call wasn't to the Church but to the police. I always wanted to be a policeman.*

He stops for a moment to relax. There's no race to remember and his memories are quiet and reflective anyway. The hands are now folded and the legs haven't moved. I ask him about going into the police force.

As a teenager you either heard the call or you didn't. My call wasn't to the Church but to the police. I always wanted to be a policeman. I suppose it's a wish fulfilment. You get to help people. Like my Dad: he helped people, too. When I got the acceptance from the police I went straight in. Fit as a flea, I was. I joined the Force as a cadet. I was eighteen – an older cadet. They did take them in at sixteen. I did the orientation in early '73. Heidelberg three months as a cadet, Eltham three months. That was where I went first. I joined the Recruit Squad at the Academy in October of '73.

He sits still, perfectly, and we take a breather, in a way. I wish I could hear a bird tweet or a knocking sound like in a radio play, but there's nothing to distract this policeman and his memory. There's a tight rhythm to his voice. It is not hushed, merely quiet – almost as though he preserves all his strength all the time, and speaking is the body's shift; like all other movement, it comes at a premium.

That form I got back, it came as an instruction from the depot. You get advised in writing, eventually, to start your recruit training. I had a sergeant ... what was his name? Atkinson, that's right. 'You're in Squad so-and-so.' 'What's drill like?'

41

He's impersonating squadron officers and this is the first real smile. It brightens everything up.

You're up first thing in the morning. New Squads had 'fatigues'. Cut the garden. Did the grass. Cleaned up all the rubbish inside. Move the stores before brekky. Run upstairs. Get showered. No sauntering along, no strolling! You walked properly. You didn't walk on to the parade ground; you'd be in big trouble if you did! 'What are you doing on my parade ground?' Extra drill. Could be an hour.

His cheeks and ears redden: the quiet, then the storm.

This was at the Old Seminary at Mount Waverley. Out there, it is. It's a big place. A pretty good mix of recruits we had, as a matter of fact. A few, there were, from Parade College.

He sighs but never shifts the big legs once the entire time we are together. He is like sculpture, the enquiring and sharpness. The never-miss-a-trick quality. Strength and astuteness. We go into learning – the academic aspects of policing.

The cleverer sorts of ones'd point you in the same direction. You got a lot of help from your squad mates. Papers were distributed. Exams, plenty of those. You studied Law and those things related to the Police Department. Spelling. How to do reporting. Language was a big part of it. There was 'the what, the who, the when, the why' (with a bigger emphasis on the 'when'). Logic is central.

You liked logic?

Logic is a very big part of it. Very helpful were the instructors. Drill instructors had to be hard. The academic part was roughly sixty per cent of training; the rest was the physical.

Camaraderie is pretty unique within the police force. When you become a copper some mates stay; others drop off. The main crux of your friends become police.

We did swimming, running. We learnt about the use of firearms. A big bit of it all was improvising. You learn such things that come very natural, such as never to give up. That's to do with your will. Camaraderie is pretty unique within the police force. When you become a copper some mates stay; others drop off. The main crux of your friends become police.

The training course was twenty-two weeks. Mine was actually longer – October '73 till April '74. I was in two squads. I was always trying to catch up. I wasn't passing exams too well. They back-squaded me three squads. I finished in the end. Out of the twenty-two, I came about eleventh.

'Which police station did you get started at?'

First place was at Russell Street. That was the first appointment. There two months ... saw a notice on the board. Went to City Traffic for eight months. Then a vacancy at Heidelberg came up. Read about that in the *Police Gazette*. I thought everyone'd go for it.

'But you got the job?'

> *You have to go in and say it slowly and properly, out of respect and compassion. The parents usually say 'Come in. Sit down, please,' and the penny has already dropped. They know something's up.*

Yeah, I was out at Heidelberg. You did your learning. You cleaned your drunks up. Shoplifting offenders had to be seen to. Cars pinched. You directed traffic. Then you went out in the van. Out into the suburbs, you went. You had to deliver death messages to people, citizens. Go round to the property, their homes, and tell them about it. There were these two brothers killed and I had to tell their Mum and Dad about it. Tell them their kids were killed. The mother, she knew what had happened in one look. By the looks on our faces. The penny'd drop when they looked through their front window and they seen the police caps on.

He wriggles and endeavours to get comfy but it isn't easy.

When it happened they were only two kilometres from where they lived. They've just gone into a tree by driving too fast, and you've got to tell their parents about it. It was late at night. You've got to just get the words out. Laurie Gaffney, my old boss at Heidelberg Police Station, used to tell us: 'Say the news in the way you'd appreciate being told yourself. Don't race through it.' He'd say, 'Don't blurt it out. It's not said in the doorway. You have to go in and say it slowly and properly, out of respect and compassion.' The parents usually say 'Come in. Sit down, please,' and the penny has already dropped. They know something's up.

There could be kids in the house: brothers, sisters. They've got to hear it, too. Sometimes you'd take a neighbour with you. It's a bit hard to tell someone on your own. If you have a good neighbour with you, they see a friend as you tell them.

A lot of police work, he explains, was seeing to things like files, no car rego paid. Debt warrants and protection orders. Restraining orders for wives to put on husbands. Then it comes – the much publicised event.

I'll never forget June of '76. I had the day off and I was on my way to my Uncle George's barber's shop in Clifton Hill. It was a Friday. There's a big intersection where High Street goes into Queens Parade. I happened to see three blokes with scarves round their faces wielding firearms. This was at the ANZ bank, the Clifton Hill one. There was a hell of a lot of noise and clatter going on. Trams banging and general frantic traffic. You can hear the trains and all from there. Everything converges there. It wasn't quiet at that hour, twenty to eleven in the morning.

He leans forward in a swivel action to keep the raspy voice going.

Cars everywhere. At the bank itself it wasn't that long after opening time. The getaway car was down the road. When I realised what was going on, I'm there – you know? Right there. At the scene where the bank robbery is going on.

He sits back creakily but the chair doesn't creak.

I pushed the hazard lights on the car. I just scooted across the road. There wasn't a service road there at the time. I had a little Mazda 808. Rammed the car into the plate glass door. There's a big bluestone step there at the entrance to the bank, then another one down. It's a fairly big drop, as a matter of fact.

Indicates this detail with his waving arms. Pulls himself back into a sort of clinch or hunch.

I've made their exit from the bank rather difficult.

Briefest, lightest, raspiest laugh.

I took 'em by surprise. They were rifling the till at the time I got there. One was fanning his gun at the staff. Lance Chee was standing on the counter. He's virtually shit himself. A few things were being said. I recall hearing 'Shoot him! Shoot him!' And 'Get him out of the way!' This bloke's saying 'Get out of here.' I'm thinking, Stick it up your arse!

His face reaches across ferociously almost on its own to show his grim determination never to surrender to criminals – even to the point of sacrifice. Never give in. He got that from the Brothers and his father.

'Go and ring the police,' I said to a passer-by who was walking past the paint shop. And he did, apparently – he went into the paint shop and rang the cops. I went back beside the car with the idea of getting out some sort of weapon. But Keith Faure, one of the robbers, came back over the counter. Keith and Norm are cousins. At the door now, they're trying to open it – kicked the glass out, then somehow the door opened because the glass was smashed. They're out on the footpath. Norm and I are trading punches. This is on the footpath, outside the bank now. One of his punches broke my nose but I got a few more good punches in. We're fighting for the jack handle – punching and fighting. Keith's somehow got himself into a doorway of Tippett's bike shop and shot me in the middle of my back. Right in the middle of it. Up high. Left shoulder blade. I don't remember the sound – only the thump.

Shows me with a jerked thumb where he got it. Swivels round in the chair to show.

I've gone down. I was awake throughout this incident. Banks have got alarms, so they've activated the silent alarms and the crooks have scampered. I heard someone bend over me to say 'Are you okay?' And I remember saying 'I'm not okay.'

A wafer of levity.

Someone got a car rug and put it over me. And they can see a bullet hole in my coat, a brown leather jacket. I heard a colleague of mine, John Tobin, say 'Mick, it'll be all right!' He said 'Just wait there and the ambulance will get here.'

'How did John Tobin look at that moment?'

He was very shocked to see someone he knew shot. The first few police who arrived took me for a member of the public because I was in casual clothes. It wasn't until John Tobin got there that they knew who I was.

'Was there a lot of blood? Yours, I mean?'

No, not a lot of blood lost at the scene. The bullet went through my left lung. It's hit the bottom knuckle of the sternum. It's done a U-turn. A spin. Its trajectory has changed.

'Is it a miracle?'

He looks unsurprised, surprised possibly about everything after such an unplanned thing where he narrowly avoided the next life. He takes a while before adding anything.

It was a nice rough ride from the ANZ Bank to the hospital. I went to St Vincent's. I felt every stone through those ambulance tyres, I can tell you that much. They drove straight down Hoddle Street, then up Victoria Parade to Saint V's. (*Although the topic is ghoulish he is just all concentration to get it right, and each letter in each word of each utterance seems like the shocks he received going over road gravel on the way to hospital.*) I said 'Enough of that' and got off the trolley. I got up and started undressing myself.

There was no exit wound. I was literally drowning in my own blood. They stuck tubes down. A pint and a half drained out of my own left lung. I was in St V's two weeks. Then ten days at the old Police Hospital on the corner of Nolan Street and St Kilda Road.

His eyes look around the bare walls for clueless descriptions of his ward in hospital twenty-three years ago. He tells of his family coming in.

Mum's upset. Police from the hospital rang Dad. He was working at Sleeman Ford at the time. They sent a police car round to my wife. I was just going to get my hair cut. Then this happened.

Eyes say isn't it amazing what life can do? Wide open, they are now. Yes it is.

It was a dying deposition I had to do, with a family vigil. This is the next day – first thing on a Saturday morning. Detectives Finlay and Douglas from the Armed Robbery Squad held up mug shots of this or that crook and I pointed him out straight away: Norm Faure. They give me the last rites. Dad told me later I nearly didn't make it.

He gravely shakes his own head, depicting his father's bedside countenance.

I'll always remember at the hospital when I was so close to death, and my family sitting in vigil right by me. Mum held my hand. Dad hung on to the bedrail. He's got his hand on top of Mum's. Mum's crying. He is, too. Six hours I was in surgery. They stitched up the left lung. They opened me up and took everything out. My surgeon was Mr Tony Wilson.

Says it in the sense that his insides are car parts.

When they've twigged there was no bullet exit wound, it was on for young and old. They cut me open to insert the drain tubes. I was awake at the time. Blood has all come out like out of hoses which are me and I'm looking on as it's happening to me. My blood was very red. That was in Casualty.

The next thirty-two months I was sick on and off. I convalesced at home. All my mates dropped over to see me. It's very close, the police force is. 'Is there anything you need?' they asked. I was twenty-one at the time. I've just turned forty-five now.

When I returned to Heidelberg in August of '76 to do light duties I had terrible pain in my back. They retired me in July of '79. Around about 1981 I felt a bit better, with the confidence to go back to work. But it took the best part of five years to do that. Do I feel hate for Norman Faure who shot me point blank? You do wonder why. That's about it, you know what I mean: Why? There was no reason to shoot me.

Awarded the George Cross medal for valour on the fourth of July in '78. Had to turn up at Government House and I've thought 'What's all this?' I didn't know what was going on. I was just told to go and see the Governor. Sir Henry Winneke was our Victorian Governor at the time and he told me I'd been awarded the George Cross medal. I got the medal on the ninth of November. It was nominated by my superiors. Everyone up to Mick Miller. Laurie Gaffney put in a report in the first place and then the request went up the chain of command to Mick Miller, then to the Premier Lindsay Thomson and so it goes. Mick Miller put his report on it. I went to London on Mothers' Day of '81. With my wife. Two of our girls have met The Queen and Queen Mother – that's one of the benefits of it, I suppose. We went to the Victoria and George Cross Association Reunion in London. Then, since that date, we go every two years.

I get headaches occasionally. I can still only sleep on my left side. It's absolutely hopeless on the right.

I did a few different jobs after it – security and so on. But I always wanted to go back to be part of the Victoria Police Force.

What happened to Norman Faure?

Norm Faure was killed in a knife fight by an inmate that he served his prison term with. The reason being that the inmate had got out first and Norm has said 'Make sure my girlfriend's alright till I get out.' What happened was the inmate moved in with Norm's girlfriend and when Norm found out on his release he's gone round there to have it out with him and knives were produced and they stabbed each other to death.

This is said matter-of-fact, without a single stress of violence or revenge or satisfaction in any way. Michael Pratt is a realist and just tells it as it is.

I left and he escorted me back to reception. My '86 Magna is again parked up the road, with its smashed back window. I drove home to my place quietened and uplifted in spirit. What a truth-teller.

From left to right: Robert, Darren, Paul, Greg, Neil, Ben, Leanne, Doug, Karen, Geoff, Phil, Shirley

The O'Loughlin Police Dynasty

Brother **Robert** (married to Shirley): Joined 1958; retired as superintendent 1988

Shirley (married to Robert): Constable 1960–62; police reservist 1976–93

Darren (son of Shirley & Robert): Joined 1983; left 1999 (detective senior constable)

Kim (daughter of Shirley & Robert): Joined early 1985; left late 1985 (constable)

Jason (son of Shirley & Robert): Joined 1990; left 1995 (constable)

Brother **Barry** (deceased): Joined 1957; deceased 1972 (detective sergeant)

Craig (son of Barry): Joined early 1984; left late 1985 (constable)

Brother **Neil:** Joined 1961; currently deputy commissioner

Paul (son of Neil; married to Karen): Joined 1991; currently detective senior constable

Karen (married to Paul): Joined 1993; currently senior constable

Brother **Geoff:** Joined 1968; currently superintendent

Leeanne & Shane (Geoff's children): Joined Police Department 1996 & 1999 respectively

Brother **Doug:** Joined 1967; currently detective superintendent

Ben (son of Doug): Joined 1997; currently constable

Greg (son of sister Sylvia – not in the force): Joined 1980; currently sergeant

All in the family

The O'Loughlin Police Dynasty

There is a regal quality about the O'Loughlin police dynasty's barbecue, you'd have to say. And why shouldn't there be? When you
consider their hierarchy, pedigree and authority, these attributes
seep through the munched chop, chopped salad and mango
cheesecake.

Up on Geoff O'Loughlin's relaxed decking at his leafy outer-
Melbourne residence you hear just about all the voices of all the
police who have ever fought for the Victorian community: a huge
and eager clan of deputy commissioners, superintendents, detectives, sergeants, senior constables, constables and a retired
policewoman – sipping tea as the salad is bunged unceremoni-
ously on paper plates and reflections are placed on the public
record.

After a long interview at Broadmeadows Police Headquarters
with Geoff and his best friend, fellow officer Michael Reeves, Geoff
invited me to this family get-together. A summoning, as it were, of
the tribe. It's like a wake, although no one has recently died. A
wake fiery as the raked-up past. Mostly serious are their tales or
chronicles, although a few light-hearted moments are evoked out
of exuberance.

My hand is shaken by several brothers, who at first glance seem
the same policeman, but after relaxing on the wooden decking
over the children's trampoline and with the drizzling rain, the
brothers seem unalike in a way I hadn't realised. Each particular
policeman has his own particular vision and idiosyncratic particular countenance. They are tough and active, and have a 'don't-
mess-with-me' look. 'Don't take me for a mug', is what the
O'Loughlins think, and it's true that they speak and react and con-
ceptualise at a rapid-fire rate. A quiet ferocity is at work not far
below their surfaces.

It's interesting to listen intently to a dynasty towards the end of
the first millennium. Indignant over some aspects of government

policy and public attitude. Outspoken on topics such as the need for unification through loyalty, and how the (albeit unlikely) prospect of commercial coppers (security officers) would produce half-hearted allegiance if they some day got the numbers on sworn officers, subjects of Her Majesty Queen Elizabeth II, although some fiercely republican. This is the grave difference between pay and soul. Perhaps the only difference.

An afternoon of service remembered and philosophy observed as the sliced celery sinks into the spoken word. The O'Loughlins are all the Queen's men, an incredible living tribe of fearless police; highly moral; full of zeal; and questioning not merely their future but the new age. They are wound up.

Over the friendly-held, thumbed-white paper-plated barbecued meats, sliced salad and a decent red, the recollections and personal moralising epithets and *bons mots* and experiences in the Force over the years travel from speakers to my listening ears. Ethics and olives. Morals and sliced-up tomatoes. The O'Loughlins are raconteur rememberers, dedicated in their tireless pursuit of justice. They are the Force, all right! All from one family. I feel privileged listening to them remembering everything.

The first of the O'Loughlins I meet is the oldest brother, Robert, retired from the police. He is gigantically casual, and introduces me to Shirley. As we shake hands, he says, 'Shirley retired in 1962 and came back as a reservist in 1976.' Then Shirley says to me, as we both sit down on the balcony, 'They get maternity leave nowadays, policewomen do; that's a huge difference.'

When did you sign up Shirley?

May of '60, at St Kilda Road Barracks, like everyone else! Selection was a process of elimination, really. A written test and then you came back in the afternoon if you passed.

She forks a sprig of fresh lettuce and smiles. Shields November slanting sun from her forehead in a feminine way.

'But what about you, Robert?'

I joined the Force in '58. Was I excited? Yeah! It's the nature of the beast. I was confident!

You look it.

Shirley waves the sprig on the fork prong and shields the sun from her eyes again. It's a bit annoying, that sun.

A lot applied – women, you know. Only four got in with our intake. It was eagerly competed for, women getting a go in the old days. And you had your height limits. Five-foot-four (that's 162.5 centimetres) was the shortest you could be. Men were taller, of course. There were a few tears about from women candidates of only five-foot-three and three-quarters ...

It must've been heartbreaking.

Geoff offers a plateful of scrumptious-looking hamburgers. 'Get that into you,' he laughs, and goes off with his wife Carol to help serve the family. He wears an Eltham Apex apron and cheerily hands out meals to the in-laws. It is hearty here. Hopeful. Strong – you can feel their strength. Confidence in the clan, of course. The power of numbers.

Robert adds to the topic of human height in respect of joining the Force:

They said, in the end, that you couldn't justify a height limit. All five-foot-five men and women suddenly got in! It was like a miracle! A lot of unnecessary distress is caused by idiotic shortsightedness!

I believe that. Shortness is my family's forté and their Waterloo. None of my lot is over five foot ten. I think I'm the tallest. I think we're Welsh.

Robert: Well, you go back to your history. 'You can't be a real policeman unless you're six foot,' they used to say. When I first joined the Uniform Branch and Wireless Patrol, if two of you walked into a pub, you had a presence. If you get two police-women of five foot they haven't got the same presence. That's what they used to say.

Shirley: There's not the same respect. Men aren't averse these days to hitting a woman.

I say 'Are there no Christian criminals left these days?' And they laugh.

Neil: Times have changed. Men now have the same height requirement as women. Size is no longer relevant.

Robert: There's been a big change of police and public attitude.

Neil: In the past, policewomen were not equipped to do general duties. They dealt with children and took rape statements. They are equal now, and so they should be.

Shirley: Now the women turn up with the men in equal number. Women officers are often better negotiators than policemen. They tend to listen better and speak more patiently. They can read the troublemaker. Men tend to react quicker, and that's not always a good thing.

Neil: In Shirley's era you had a separate policewoman's list with specific duties, such as 'Child Protection and Shoplifting'. When you went out in the Divvy Van in the 60s the women would just be a back-up. In the current environment it can be two policewomen in a Divvy Van and they deal with it; they deal with anything. They have to!

It's only fitting that I am introduced at this point to Neil's daughter-in-law, Karen, who has something to say on the matter:

Females are expected to be as competent as their male work-mates, and rightly so. Females in general have voiced their right to equal opportunity for years and it's only fair that this should be evident in the police force. I wouldn't say it's more dangerous nowadays; it's just that we seem to be more involved than in Shirley's day, when I guess females were expected to care for children or work behind a desk and not drive the van.

Shirley: We were after a stolen car once, I remember. I remember a bridge, where was that now? The gardens are there, too. Oh, yeah, Batman Avenue. We found him lying doggo like Moses in the bullrushes.

Shirley laughs. Me too. Haven't heard 'doggo' before.

Robert: If you're going to a job and know what to expect, that's one thing. You just deal with that as it comes up. And you know to an extent what to expect. If you're a policeman, your expectations are entirely different [from those of ordinary citizens]. The most dangerous call you'd get is a domestic. Trouble at such-and-such-a-place. It could be major or minor. You don't know.

Neil: Domestics in the past were drink-related. Now they're drug-related, far more dangerous, but police are better trained now.

Geoff: Drugs are the curse of our society. Governments throughout the world have failed to address this huge problem adequately. Users will do anything to get their fix. They have no choice; they are addicted. I had a user break his grandmother's finger trying to get her ring off to sell it. It is hard to give that person compassion, after speaking to, and seeing what happened to, grandma.

One of the biggest problems that the police force and the community have today is that family values have broken down.

Neil: There were and there still are important great family values. As children we'd be playing in the street. You'd see, as a kid, an elderly neighbour with a heavy bag in her hand, and without stopping to think about anything at all, you'd go over to her and carry her bag home. One of the biggest problems that the police force and the community have today is that family values have broken down. For instance, people in general don't go to church as much as they used to.

That's true. They don't go much today. I never do, though I think I will.

Neil adds: We are recruiting from the community so we get officers who have current community values. The good and the bad.

Geoff leans on my shoulder and murmurs.

In the world of equal opportunity you can't differentiate. Providing their personal beliefs are lawful. Nothing we can do about anyone's personal choices. It's entirely up to them, these days.

    Neil: It's not an easy occupation being in the police force. And it's the image of the police force we have to take into consideration as well as that of the individual's background.

> *The Victorian Force is a billion-dollar business. If we don't keep up with the latest changes, we'll just fall behind. We need the latest technology to keep ahead of the crooks.*

Robert: Within the Force there'll always be an element of hard liners who look upon themselves as an island. Policing's not only about law and order. Policing's about people as well.

    Neil: Policing, these days, is not about cops and robbers. It's a business – a billion-dollar business, OK? If we don't keep up with the latest changes, we'll just fall behind. We need the latest technology to keep ahead of the crooks. We still need to personalise the efforts of the members by thanking them or rewarding them. Perhaps we don't do that enough.

What do the public want: part-time basic protection or fully trained professionals? Their choice.

Geoff butts in: But we are learning. In Victoria currently there are about 23,000 security guards and only 10,000 fully trained sworn members. If the community push their politicians for more police, saying we need more to feel safer, they'll get them from their politicians. The community as a whole are the only ones that can demand and get more fully trained professional police – not security guards with limited skill and basic training. Security guards have a limited role and private enterprise pays for them. Police have to play a vast number of roles. What do the public want: part-time basic protection or fully trained professionals? Their choice.

Doug, who was a member of the Special Operations Group (SOG) for seventeen years, says:

If the community accepts private security guards they'll put them out en masse with guns on their hips in two weeks. Constables have to make decisions on the spot all the time for about $45,000 a year, all up, and the judiciary who sit in judgement on our decisions and performance can take their time to make a final judgement. The judiciary, like police, would have difficulty getting it right all the time, especially if they had to make a decision in the same time frame. But they would argue they made the decision in good faith. So do we! We are the only business in Australia that has to work like that.

I remember once, when I was in the SOG, I was at a family

twenty-first birthday party in Doncaster and I was on call. It was a Saturday night. There was a siege in Altona North at about 10 pm. I left the party (sober) to attend to the siege and returned three hours later. One of my cousins, who was in the computer industry, had me explain what had happened. I told him that a bloke was threatening to kill himself and everyone around him. He asked how much I got for being called out on a Saturday night. I told him I was an officer, so I received nothing extra. He said he was on $120 an hour, and triple time for Saturday. When I told him what I earned per week he couldn't believe that was what I was paid for such dangerous and responsible work. I told him I didn't join for the money. I was standing with my brothers at the time and they just nonchalantly nodded. I remember the look of disbelief on my cousin's face. He just didn't understand. Didn't want to.

Geoff: My nephew Darren, a good policeman working in the computer crime department, has just accepted a job as an expert in a computer security firm. He was offered twice the pay to leave the police. The Force rely on your dedication and that pressures you to stay, but you've got a family; you can't eat allegiance.

It's a hard philosophical conundrum this, it certainly seems. Do you cling to your job in the Force or go where the pickings are riper elsewhere?

Take the public – who really seem to take the police for granted (unless it is them personally who require help, that is) – it's a Utopian concept, but I wonder whether they might not come out in the street in a show of rare strength with placards and so on declaring their love of the Force: 'WE LOVE OUR VICTORIA POLICE FORCE!' Is it possible? They'd never do a thing like that, out of apathy.

Geoff concludes and sees to the hamburgers. They're bloody nice – I can't get them to taste like that. I can just overhear him above the snag steam as he hands out extra chops behind me saying, 'You talk to any of the victims and the majority of them have nothing but praise for us.'

Paul, Neil's son and Karen's husband, has a turn now.

It's so funny to listen to you guys comparing the past with today. Karen and I weren't even born in the 1960s!

'Why did you join, Paul?' I ask him, eager for an insight into the formation of the dynasty.

I think hearing the often interesting and funny stories told around the family table certainly made it appealing. But I would have to say the most important factor was, and still is, the tremendous pride and respect I always felt towards my father and my uncles. I believe that, in a world where both moral and family values are decreasing the Victoria Police and the O'Loughlin family tradition truly stand out as an example of what should be important to people.

Paul and Karen met at Broadmeadows Police Station, where they both worked, their fathers once having worked together in the Armed Robbery Squad.

Karen: Actually, there's a story to tell about the first time Paul and I were working together, she volunteers. We attended a 'domestic' between a senile old lady and her husband. The lady was prone to wandering off, and her husband was trying to stop her. She called the police because she had forgotten the male was her husband.
Sounds like Alzheimer's ...

Paul explained to the lady that it wasn't safe to walk the streets of Broadmeadows on her own, because she was at risk of being injured or becoming lost. He explained to her, for example, that I was working with him to protect him, and vice versa. She took this the wrong way and told us what a lovely couple we were. Five months later we were engaged!

I ask her 'What pressures had been placed on you to join? Any?'

I joined because of family influence – saw the achievements of my father and uncle and was proud of the work they did and wanted to do the same. I was under no pressure to join – in fact, father tried to talk me out of it.

You are definitely altered once you become a sworn member.

Shirley comes to sit next to me as I scoop up life-giving lettuce. My little son Louis is boing-ing on the O'Loughlin trampoline down there beneath the decking, and it's stopped raining now. It's lovely here and the day plods bluely along. With a little patience we can learn about our tribe. They are our protectors, surely to God.

Shirley: The public's feeling for us is sometimes hard to get onto. One thing's for certain – you are definitely altered once you become a sworn member.

Robert: Dad always said 'You have to be 110 per cent squeaky clean if you want to be a policeman.' That's a high standard to maintain and you lose friends along the way because they can't cope with the standard.

If I can help even half a dozen people I'll be more than happy.

Shirley: As a protector you know what to do at any time. I have a love of people rather than a love of the public. I suppose love's in the miniature. You just do what you think you should do in any isolated, small circumstance, rather than try to help the whole State of Victoria.

What it is with me – if I can help even half a dozen people I'll be more than happy. You don't feel pleased with yourself exactly. No, that's not it, that's not the feeling, my feeling. It could've been you, in a terrible condition or a terrible jam. Down and out and desperate for help from the police. It's very much a 'There but for the grace of God' kind of thing.

I remember an old whore who once sat, with no pants on, in the drain. In St Kilda, I think it was. St Kilda it was, for sure. It could only happen in St Kilda. When I questioned her as to what she was up to, she said to me – and I remember exactly the way she said it, too – 'Oh, just giving it an airing, that's all, love! Just an airing, see!'

She laughs like mad and I am temporarily stunned. God, they really see everything in life – the grotesque and the normal, all mixed up. It's a crude tale but a good one, certainly. I can just see one of the whores saying that, from my own memories of Fitzroy Street.

Greg is an O'Loughlin nephew, the son of Sylvia, the eldest of three O'Loughlin sisters. He agrees with his auntie:

The good feeling you get when you have helped someone makes it all worthwhile. But some of the funny incidents help. For a young man like me with a fairly sheltered upbringing, working at the Licensing, Gaming and Vice squad in the early 1980s was a real education. I recall having to work one New Year's Eve. We went and did the rounds of the brothels/massage parlours in the St Kilda and South Melbourne areas. As we were leaving one, our exit was blocked by a six-foot blond transsexual insisting on a New Year's kiss. Now, there are only so many sacrifices one can be expected to make for the job. Quoting the applicable offence cleared the way out! The job has the scope for more unusual incidents than any other I can think of. But you also have to have a sense of humour to cope with the realities of life that it throws at you.

Being young, too, Paul picks up on the humourous side of things:

Once I was interviewing a person arrested for using cannabis. When asked the obligatory question 'Are you licensed under the Drugs Poisons and Controlled Substances Act to possess or use cannabis?' the offender leapt to his feet and yelled in a very animated fashion 'Licensed? You can be licensed? How do I get a licence?'

Ben, Paul's cousin and often a colleague on the job, joins in:

Yeah. It's always exciting. Never the same two days running. Even if the paperwork is R.S. Once, Paul and I had a funny experience – well, quite embarrassing really. On night shift one night at Broady we were called to deal with a drunk lying out cold on someone's front lawn. Paul went for his shoulders and I went for the legs, trying to pick him up and carry him to the van. As we lifted, he fell apart – literally. I stood there with his legs in my hands (the legs were prosthetic), while the rest of him was still on the lawn, with Paul at the other end.

Everyone laughs, then Doug injects a note of sobriety: A lot of policing is very satisfying, it really is. It's just that we aren't paid enough for the responsibility we have, compared with other professions. Look at what we do. I've spent a lot of time at the Coroner's Court explaining my actions. Sometimes you're 'damned if you do and damned if you don't'! But you accept and get on with your job. They've got all the time in the world to sit in judgement on what we do in a matter of seconds. What do they know about active policing, being face to face with life-threatening situations?

It's 6 pm and getting freezing cold out on the decking, so we go indoors for a respite, a rest. All of the clan are washing dishes and chatting amiably as kids (the next generation of a police dynasty?) sit or laugh or endeavour to descend steps to the basement for a look-see. I sit next to Geoff and he says:

Everything changes. In the '70s, both the community and the police attitude to drink driving was very lax – remember? Entirely different now. It is not tolerated, and the police attitude is in line with the public's. That's the way it should be: police attitude is a reflection of the community. We don't tolerate drink driving either.

Robert says: Unfortunately our brother Barry was killed in a car accident and consequently he's not here, or else we'd be just about intact as a clan. He got an unbelievable send-off, don't worry about that.

Geoff adds: So did Fred (a brother-in-law, also a cop – Barry's best friend). Two great cops – two of the best, it's the uncertainty of the job that makes it fantastic but also makes it dangerous. A 45-year-old superintendent got shot at recently.

Doug O'Loughlin tells me about the mother of a shot offender who thanked the members involved by letter. She said in the letter she knew her son was dangerous and would kill them (the family) and she realised the danger and difficulty the members had in taking the action they did (killing him).

It is gratifying to get a letter like that. It helps you cope. Actually, I went and saw her. Had a cup of tea.

He remembers police shootings and the inevitability of them. 'No police officer wants to kill any member of the public,' he says in a whisper. Neil agrees:

You have a basic obligation to protect yourself and the public. If you do get shot at it is of little consequence thinking 'Why did I let that happen?'

Geoff: I remember being called to an 'offender's on' – possible shots fired on night shift. I was thirty-four, two kids, mortgage. I climbed up onto the roof. I saw someone hiding behind a chimney. I thought he had a gun in his hand – it was a bangle on his wrist, gleaming in the moonlight. I called for him to 'drop the gun'. He didn't. I remember actually taking up the pressure on the trigger. Luckily he put his hands up, so I didn't have to shoot. (I had nowhere to go – that was my only option.) I was so wild with him because no one would have believed me; I may have had to leave my job and lose everything. It turns out he was only sixteen.

Doug confirms how common this is:

That happened to me on a SOG raid. The offender, who was wanted for murder, sat up in bed, pointing his hand at us as though he had a gun. I suppose it's the training. You focus on the hands. Most times it works – hands kill!

Someone in the background says, tongue in cheek, 'But we knew the job was dangerous when we took it.'

The O'Loughlins couldn't have been much more open to me and my little family, and I left their sincerity and charms and monologues with a new outlook on not just cops but much, much more. Life, death, duty, and – you'd have to say – the recognition of the family as everything.

Geoff says, as we head for the car and waves: 'Hope it hasn't been too heavy for you, Barry. We could talk shop forever. It's a great clan, ours.' Indeed it is. And so the long talk is over. I wished we did this every Sunday. We might have a unified community after all. Instead of feeling all broken up.

It's good to come from a clan. It is the one fundamental family that is unified.

Charles Pilgrim
Joined Victoria Police 1938
Retired as sergeant 1968

An honest veteran

Charles Pilgrim – 86-year-old retired sergeant

It proved more than elusive endeavouring to track down Charles Pilgrim, the stoic constable of eighty-six summers and endless 1930s police 'beats'. His home seemed to have no physical number on it. The house beside his one was number 778, its number easy enough to make out, but Charles's home seemed quite numberless. Presuming it to be 776, I knocked at the front door. No one answered. Not wanting to be a nuisance, I wandered around the enormous front yard like a man on a mission. Gigantic bulbs and enormous roses nodded sagely in the truant September breeze. The day hummed and whistled – innocently enough. You couldn't question the day.

Eventually I went into the garage beside the house, hoping there was no Rottweiler there to have a go at me. There was a car and crates and boxes and tins of paint going nowhere, but no ancient retired policeman anywhere to be seen. I played around with the latch on the rustic garden gate and a man's voice bellowed 'Come in. We're out here now!' I wondered where they used to be.

Although pretty hobbledy, Charles managed to get up and escort me inside his spacious residence.

Mr Pilgrim's huge body reclined in a kind of geared easychair. He was stout, and looked fit apart from a baffling kind of aluminium fluted walking cane, which he swang in the air as a gesture of friendliness. He had on olive-coloured winter-weight slacks and a mustard-coloured very thick woollen cardigan. His wife was not well and smiled sheepishly behind a screwed-up floral hankie. She was very thin indeed and just about asleep, all curled up in the corner of a living-room that was musty, thick with dust and filled with 1930s and 40s porcelain vases as well as romantically inclined heroic landscapes.

Charles Pilgrim was neither jovial nor theatrical, merely a time traveller. He waved the fluted walking-cane in an indication that I should begin the interview. I had to sit up close to his ears to speak to him.

'Where do you come from?'

Saint Arnaud. Born on the sixth of December 1913, to Charles William Herbert and Beatrice Pilgrim, at Marnoo East, twenty-five miles from Saint Arnaud. Dad was a farmer. Great-grand-father William got there in 1853. Lived there ever after. Breeders of Clydesdale horses. Lincoln and Leicester sheep. Which he exhibited and later judged. This is my grandfather. He was a horse judge.

A stern, judicious glance through his thick spectacles. As if to say 'Are you with me?' I am, Charles. Right with you, old chap.

He also judged horses at The Royal Show. He once said to me at the Perth Show: 'There are ten horses here for every one in Melbourne.'

This thought or reminiscence appears current, as though a friendly or particularly kind grandfatherly ghost is standing by his easychair, nodding to him.

As a boy I loved the farm life. Walk a mile to get to a horse to ride, rather than ride a bike or anything else. They know you personally. (*Kicks his feet up.*)

Mrs Pilgrim says they had difficulty finding their own street number because the council made those numbers out of lead long ago and set them into the footpath when the cement was getting paved, but kids pinched that lead to sell it to scrap metal dealers in the area and that's why it was hard to find them. I thanked her and she says 'That's all right' and then closes her eyes again and curls up in a ball in her corner chair and falls asleep straight away.

There was a horse I gave a switch to once called Cactus. Alice, Paddy, Rose – we had a lot of horses in those days – and Stella, my father's particular favourite.

I wonder what your his social memories are, of having fun in the old days.

Well, I went round the dance hall floor at four years of age. Lorna (*gesturing towards his wife*) and I won a waltzing competition.

'You were so young when you met?'

The school I attended was Marnoo East State School. Some few years ago, they decided to put up a stone memorial (*his hands describe a memorial stone*) to every school that has gone and been forgotten. I had to give a little talk recently up that way. I told them school was four miles on a horse and gig. Many years later, long after the school had closed, there I was, unveiling that memorial. Because of the mixed ages there were few fights after school. Three or four kids to each class but everyone in the same room, that's how it was.

'Were you tough?'

I don't think so. Robust boy, I was. Drank fresh milk. I could milk a cow when I was five. (*His huge hands show milking action.*) I milked a cow in Glen Waverley for twelve years, which is here, where we still live. Plenty of clover in Glen Waverley in those days. So rich in the spring the kids said 'You'd better put the separator on. It's too strong, the milk!'

Too rich! Give you spots!'

'Water it down, Dad!' they used to say. Some people drank it as soon as it come in.

'Were you a worshipful boy?' He seems like one, now, with such a wide-open countenance.

I was taken to Marnoo Presbyterian Church when I was four years old. I just went – too young to express an opinion. In the country there was not much time for debating. It was work, work, work!

I boarded privately and went to the High School. When I was twelve to about fifteen I went to the C of E and I pumped the organ and sang. As for punishment at our little country school, I can't recall the strap being used. There was just the one room where we all were. In the morning, the parents brought the wood. It went in the hearth, to be lit by the teacher. Everything was on the blackboard. Emphasis on English and spelling, mental arithmetic.

Left school – let's see – I was away at boarding school three years. I was fifteen when I left. I never got 'the call' to go to church. There was a man there who said if we would put our faith in Christ, we'd go through the world. One Sunday he fell out of the pulpit. He used to get carried away and so on. He said of Jesus 'You might be hungry but you'll never starve.' That priest was called Clinch. (*His teeth snap satisfactorily as he pronounces 'Clinch'. He suddenly runs out of puff and is just a sweet man in a chair.*)

I can't get up and down now, you see?

But I *was* a practising Christian, in the bush. One of many.

His body is quietly rocking and cradling the memories, and his monumental paws are clasped hard without twiddling. He's like stone. A sculpture of an ancient copper. He doesn't blink. Looks every onward, on duty.

I was in the church vestry when I was eighteen – used to take up the collection. I can tell you that in 1938 (which was when I went to Fitzroy and joined the police force), the plate came round and all you'd see was no end of halfpennies. Not too many deeners. My task was to administer these funds. I was entrenched in the goings-on of this church and my work was to make sure the collection was properly taken care of.

How did I get the calling to join the police? Times were very bad. The Depression was tough. On the streets of Fitzroy, you'd see little skinny kids asking for a penny. 'Can you give me a penny?' they'd cry out. They were sent out by their parents but they were the ones begging. They were sent out to get money for drink. Sometimes I let them keep that coin so long as they really spent it on bread to eat, a crust – not drink for their mum and dad, and they'd sometimes agree.

I was working for my foster parents up at Belgrave – Tecoma, really – when I came down to Melbourne to sit for the police exam. A full 220 hopefuls turned up for it.

'You would've romped that in, Charles, wouldn't you, being so robust?'

I romped it in, all right! One hundred and eighty were left – a quarter of them didn't make it through the physical test and they just sat for the written exam. A lot of the young blokes looked scrawny. Their ages ranged from nineteen to twenty-six-ish. But you didn't know straight away whether you'd been accepted by them. No, you got a notification through the post if you were successful. That's right! When my mother died in 1936 I left home and joined the police force. Dad remarried and he was working on a farm in the capacity of caretaker.

Lorna wakes briefly and squints at Charles, then tucks her knees up higher yet, and falls asleep again. I wouldn't mind a doze as well. Maybe we're all asleep.

My mum had cancer. I wrote to my father once a week when I was in Tecoma. Dad would reply, beautifully. He wrote to me with such care, and in a beautiful hand. Young people of today have no idea what effort parents put into the letters to their children in the old days. Those letters were eagerly looked forward to. I don't think I spoke to Dad much in twenty years ... it was all in the letter writing.

The first station I worked in, when I joined the Force, was on the corner of Condell and Napier streets in Fitzroy. About eight of us lived upstairs above the station. We had a communal shower with plenty of hot water – more than you got outside.

He stares ahead at items on the historic dining table: cups, saucers, and teaspoons. Outside, there are birds singing and a man clomps in noisily to speak briefly to Charles about something. They chat and smile, then the man departs and Charles grins as he talks of what coppers used to munch back in the Depression years at Fitzroy Police Station.

We used to eat! At the barracks about two days a week, we ate! Plenty of stews. Mutton, cabbage, carrots. It was good! Sizzled it up ourselves! On night duty.

I started on eight pounds eight a fortnight, of which two pounds two was taken for board at the Police Depot at St Kilda Road. (*More rocking. I'm hoping he will not fall backwards out of this strange swaying chair.*) See that you done all the work. That's what you had to do. They give you an old-fashioned hat, made of stiffened black material.

Lorna sighs. Birds twitter. The sun comes through. Where are you Charles? Can you hear me or the birds calling?

Guns were held at the desk. You could get a gun if your request was reasonable. (*He looks at me as if to say 'It might take all day.'*)

You did twenty-two weeks' training. You got the Silver Baton at the end of it. I was Dux of the intake, that's why I got the Silver Baton. For the intelligence as much as the fitness. For some of the physical training you were allowed to go in shorts. You'd lay on the floor. There'd be marks from your body. Perspiration marks: legs, arms, back. They had it all worked out what you had to do.

> *You had to have plain-toed shoes, which you paid thirteen and six for, out of your own pay.*

Then there'd be eight laps of the oval to warm up. You had to tread the 'beat'. The beat was the distance between two spots where you had to walk on your police rounds. You had to have plain-toed shoes, which you paid thirteen and six for, out of your own pay. They didn't *give* them to you! For anyone who could afford special shoes there was Kangaratta Shoes. (*He slowly spells out 'Kangaratta' and closes his eyes to see and sniff them again.*)

The rules of the beat were simply that you had to walk and you weren't allowed to go off that beat. There were various beats, such as Brunswick Street, Smith Street and Nicholson Street. We didn't walk Gore Street though. We walked along where the shops were. Gertrude Street, that was tough. There was a woman who used to get drunk, and she wouldn't walk! She'd lay down and kick and scream – with no pants on. (*He looks both bemused and appalled.*) She looked terrible – a funny little old thing. A few Aborigines were around. And those bloody Murphys – that family was terrible. They were terrible people.

Rubs his large enquiring eyes with the backs of the great palms and blinks, but there's no tiredness or water or anything weary in his big open eyes. It's as if the eyes that speak and remember everything he's seen are all there is of him now. He's in the past and the present.

Mrs Murphy, she didn't have much of a conscience. Round the corner in Fitzroy Street, between two and three in the morning, she took her thirteen-year-old daughter, you know. I knew half of the staff there on duty. I'd get a call. 'That's a brothel!' I'd scream.

I went round there to that brothel and the woman I saw was forty or so. She had a black bloke on her when I went in. Of course he wanted to roll all over her for five shillings. But she wouldn't do anything. He was six foot six. I had me baton with me. I said 'Get out!' Then she screamed at him to get out. I seen her get hold of a chair. That was the end of him. I had a torch with me.

My work was mostly to deal with drunks or kids misbehaving in the streets. I had to rely on me tongue to get out of trouble. If I got into trouble, some little kid'd run to the police station and yell 'Charlie's in trouble!' And then I'd be all right. Everything would be all right, again, you see?

Lorna again awakens and gazes wearily around the darkening room, as the sun at the back of their enormous rear garden tiptoes behind a big white cloud. It's like being with old, rare children. They're so precious!

I was able to save a little money in the old days. I was at my grandfather's the night war was declared. We heard Menzies' speech on radio. I'd got engaged that very weekend. I just went straight back to the barracks. A lot of them wanted to join the Army, but you couldn't if you were with the police. It caused some grief, as a lot of them wanted to serve their country. A mate, Roy, said he'd join anyway. So he resigned and got killed immediately in England. A letter of his, I got after he died – just after. I was a copper all through the war. The Second One.

Time is not going anywhere. Time isn't interested in interrupting the present. A gift of time, are Charles's stories. I have come to listen to him defy time.

I went to the Criminal Investigation Branch at Russell Street next. The old grey building at the back. I was a constable. Melbourne had a brown-out during the war. The Second One.

He never tires. I just realised it. He's indefatigable. I wouldn't mind a rest but he's as fresh as a daisy, on his clover. Time just drifts, with an old copper hanging on to its ticking tone. History seems to be something akin to picking up a live phone, and the old brain-boxing memory jumps.

> *I applied for the job of Cadet Instructor down at St Kilda Road. Missed out – as the former Silver Baton winner. It would've changed my whole life if I'd got it.*

The American throttler Leonski was hanging around Royal Park in the war years. I was aware of him. He was living near the zoo. The daily load was just keys out and into the hurly-burly. I got into the clerical side of it. As a matter of fact, I applied for the job of Cadet Instructor (CI for short) down at St Kilda Road. Missed out – as the former Silver Baton winner. It would've changed my whole life if I'd got it.

No clinching of lips. He's never sorry for himself. His right palm is doing all the drama now, folding its thumb and joints of thick banana-like fingers for expression.

I did my detective training course at the CI Branch. Retired in 1969. Thirty-one years in the police force with one week's sick leave – and that was a bad cold. (*He pats his cold pale, broad forehead.*) As a teetotaller, I woulddnt've had a party. In 1945 I was temporarily seconded to Vic Railways. Stolen smokes at Dynon

Road, that sort of thing. It was rife in the railways – thieving, I tell you what.

I ask him whether you must be a good judge of character to be a policeman.

There were offences such as Loitering with Intent to Commit a Felony, which you can see coming in their face and eyes. You know they're going to commit one, all right, and it's your job to stop it. Crims needed priors (meaning prior convictions) to go to jail. I never felt hatred for any of them. Not crims who'd just drifted a bit from the straight-and-narrow. I knew how to talk to them. I was accepted by them. I knew them all. My colleagues used to say 'Send Charlie in to cry with them!'

You'd get under their skin. You understood perfectly the way to break someone – with persistent questioning in their own language. Actually, my staff couldn't get admissions, but I could. You'd never ever say you knew what they'd done. Never accuse them of something they might not have done. It was a matter of complete trust to get a confession out of them.

When I was in the Transit Police, the boys brought a fellow to me off the train from Sydney one day. They reckoned he'd stolen thirty pounds off another passenger. We can't see anyone else. I can't get a lead. So I said 'Strip off!' And he took off all of his clothes, including his shoes and socks, and I noticed something funny about one of his socks. There was this little wad sticking out of it. That was where the money was!

He laughs and is instantly on the beat again.

At Montague Shipping Yards one time I said to another suspect 'Strip off!' And this chap was wearing three pair of pink ladies' bloomers. He was about twenty and just did as he was told. He did twelve months for it. He was already on a bond, and he'd broken it, you see.

The crims weren't so much petty crims as good crims, the ones I was lenient with. Some of them said the only reason they weren't in jail was that they told the truth. I always gave them the benefit of the doubt.

Any corruption was unknown to me, because I was known as an honest cop.

'*Was there any corruption in the police when you were there?*'

Any corruption was unknown to me, because I was known as an honest cop. Put this at the end. (*His eyes blaze.*)

He very painfully gets up out of the jarring easychair to climb the old floral carpeted stairs of his home. I give him a hand and realise just how big he is. He had begun to look like a small man in the chair but now that he is up he is huge and square. After an eternity he comes back down the steps again, right out of puff. He shows me an old dark blue crushed velvet box with a tiny hard silver baton in it complete with its own bizarre twirly bit of tassel.

Fourteen of us lined up to get one of these. (*He puffs, and his eyes are full.*) When the Second War come, they stopped giving them out. The last one was in '42. Then it was reinstated in '90 I think.

I hold the object up and inspect its intricate description: 'Baton Of Honour. Won By Constable Charles William James Pilgrim No. 9243 5-7-38'.

He then props in his kitchen and I sit there with him, with the telephone and the stove and flowers freshly snipped from his garden. He rubs his jaw and says he forgets who I am. Lorna has Alzheimer's, he says, then adds: 'Me, too, a bit. But not as bad.'

He shows me to the back wicker gate and we shake hands. He says he still drives his car to the shops.

Give us a ring and we'll talk again.

Colleen Woolley

1965–72 with South Australian and New South Wales police

Joined Victoria Police 1976

Retired as senior sergeant, due to ill-health, 1992

Now with the Retired Police Association

Maybe we could make a difference

Colleen Woolley – retired senior sergeant

In salubrious Carlton, where it's the height of fashion to sip caffe latte leisurely as you back-stab an old colleague and request an expensive two-metre menu containing squab or obscure lettuces, here is Colleen Woolley, a retired police officer who has given her life to better the lot of retired police officers.

It is a very great relief to listen to somebody interesting after a lifetime of bores in Carlton and I notice the friendly and reassuring quality of retired Senior Sergeant Woolley's voice. She gives me a copy of *Arresting Women*, a history of women in the Victoria Police containing recollections and rare snapshots of women who joined the Force in times gone by. She signs the book with a flourish and starts telling me such beginnings of anecdotes that they beguile me and quietly appal me. I ask whether we can meet again at a quiet pub and 'speak of everything' over a grogless luncheon. 'Sure,' she says. And a week later, in between lamb of the day and a few pots of lemon squash, she sits with me at the Brandon Hotel in Station Street, Carlton, and puts me in the picture.

She's big and strong; she's been through everything. As well as these attributes, I am struck by her love of her workmates; she would willingly die for her friends in the Force, for whom she has given all. Her voice is strong and unhesitating. Very direct. It is a no-stuffing-around voice. A bright voice. Sharp. Restless.

There were so many things that arose the other day, when we had coffee, that I'd like to collect some of the stories, if that's all right. For example, you told me about being personally assaulted. What were the circumstances of that episode?'

Well, there were several episodes. One probably distressed me more than the others, because a male colleague who was with me just stood back and watched a whole family assault me. He was scared because he was very new and just didn't know what to do.

It was a very quiet Sunday morning on the streets of Preston. This young rookie and I had pulled in to a side street and had seen a taxi sitting at the kerb with the engine running. In areas like Preston, leaving a vehicle unattended and running is inviting someone to commit a crime, apart from the fact that it's illegal in itself. So we managed to ascertain quickly where the driver was: it turned out that he had just popped in home to pick something up. When I cautioned him he became very belligerent. Then, as we were walking back towards the cab to get a few details, the man's family decided they weren't going to have the head of the household taken to task by a policewoman and they all decided that they would have a go. I had him struggling with me in front, the wife belting me from behind, and the kids all jumping up and down and trying to get in on the act. And the rookie policeman, who would have been in his late teens or early twenties, just froze.

It wasn't a serious assault, but I was getting concerned because it could have very, very quickly got out of hand. What was occurring was bad enough, but the lack of support made it fairly traumatic. In the end I just screamed at him 'Call for back-up!' and when I screamed at him he finally functioned. But after that he just stood there again; he didn't know what to do while we were waiting for back-up to arrive.

'And how did it all end?'

As soon as a few more uniforms turned up the whole family became very good little citizens again. He was charged with minor assault and one traffic offence.

Then there was one time at Russell Street when I was assaulted by a young woman. In police work you end up restraining or trying to restrain a lot of mentally ill people. I mean I've got dozens of anecdotes about mental patients. Some of them are absolutely hilarious and some of them are really sad.

My assailant was a temporal lobe epileptic in her early twenties, who hadn't been taking her medication. She had been drinking grog and had also been smoking pot. She came into the area where I was working (at the public help desk area, as a media liaison officer) and passed out. When I went to give her first aid she looked up and came to, and came to fighting – she looked up and saw me and just started lashing out. All I could do was to try to restrain her but she had the strength of ten people. Any police officer or any health worker will tell you that people like that get this superhuman strength and you don't know where it comes from. I've seen tiny little old ladies needing five big people to restrain them, and that's with Valium pumping through their bloodstream.

I was with this girl on my own for nearly a minute before help arrived. It was only by chance that the sergeant in another reception area heard the thumping and came in. It eventually took seven men to get her over to the watch house. She actually broke her arm in the process and didn't know about it till the next day.

'Do you think that there might be a perception amongst the public that the police don't converse with these people properly?'

Well, you can't. It's impossible to. When I was at Heidelberg, there was one girl in her mid-30s. She was one of the most beautiful women I have ever seen. She spoke five or six languages. She was highly, highly intelligent, beautifully dressed, beautifully groomed – and as mad as a cut snake. It was back in the days when we were in Women Police Divisions and didn't have guns or handcuffs or batons or anything – we just had our skirts to protect us, sort of thing. We were called to this house, another policewoman and I, and when we got there, this girl was brandishing a tag off a washing machine. According to her that was the key to the world and you had to repeat, time and again, the phrase 'Rover take over.' She told us 'Rover is going to take over and this is his key.' So we talked to her for a little while and then we thought, 'She's gotta go'. With a great deal of trouble we got her out to the car.

On the way to hospital she flipped out of it and she said 'I am so sorry. I can see what is happening, but I can't do anything to control it. I really apologise, I don't mean to hurt you.' I said, 'That's okay. We just want to get some help for you. Obviously you need help.'

At the hospital the doctor came in to interview her and we were both standing there, with her still lucid. We thought, 'Oh, he's not going to certify her because she's still being lucid and, you know, answering all these questions.' 'Yes, I know what day of the week it is. I know what my name is ...' da-da-da-da-da-da. All of a sudden she lent over to the doctor, picked at his white coat and said 'Oh, pubic hair! You've been sucking a vagina!' I've never seen a doctor fill out papers so quickly in all my life. (*She roars with crackly laughter.*)

We had all sorts of trouble with her. I think that was at the Austin and we had to get her up to Larundel. The damage she caused between the two hospitals was just astonishing. She even tried to jump out of the car. In the end, she and I were sprawled in this ungodly tangle in the back, me with my legs over her and arms around her, trying to restrain her. I stayed like that until we got there and my colleague went in to grab some help.

You have to strike up a rapport with strangers –
including children and old people and all sorts of
people. Anyone who decides to become a police officer
has an innate sense of community anyway ... Also, you
have to be a good negotiator, you've got to have a great
sense of humour, you've got to have the wisdom of Job,
the patience of God – forbearance. You've got to have a
strong stomach sometimes.

The skills you need to have as a police officer are considerable, when you think of how many there are – the tasks. You're a social worker ...'

Sure. You have to strike up a rapport with strangers – including children and old people and all sorts of people. Anyone who decides to become a police officer has an innate sense of community anyway ... But the girl who walked in and passed out could have had all sorts of problems. I mean she may well have been diabetic and things could have been totally different. You can't afford to take things at face value.

Also, you have to be a good negotiator, you've got to have a great sense of humour, you've got to have the wisdom of Job, the patience of God – forbearance. You've got to have a strong stomach sometimes – a very strong stomach. I could never be a nurse ... God, I admire what they do.

In my day the women in the police force always carried a bit of perfume or eau de cologne, so that when you went into certain houses you could put it over your nose because otherwise you would be heaving all over the place. I can remember going to one outer Melbourne suburb and stepping into the worst place I had ever been in. The smell was atrocious. There were faeces and things all over the floor and the dishes hadn't been done for ages, the stove was covered in filth ... You know, you wouldn't have put a dog in there. And in the corner *there* was the television – these people might not have decent clothes or anything else but there's always the television in the corner!

There had been a complaint from neighbours that the kids weren't well treated and that sort of thing, so we had gone out to investigate. We found two boys, one about three and the other still a babe in arms, in a truly shocking state. The babe in arms was covered in soil – he was absolutely filthy. To pick him up, you know ... you really didn't want to have to do it, but you had no choice. The smell in this house was appalling, the feel of the children was appalling.

What always used to get to me was that, if you pinched the skin of kids like this, it stayed in that pinch for a long time before it went back and that's what these kids were like. With normally hydrated people like us, when you pinch the skin, it just pops back. When you're malnourished and dehydrated it doesn't. (*She pinches her left wrist to show me the effect.*)

Anyway we decided that there was nothing for it but to put these two children on a Protection Application and take them away from their parents. We took the whole family back to the Heidelberg women police office and, for the first of only two times in my career, I actually had to tear a child from its parent's arms. This is an awful thing to have to do. The child is crying and all you want to do is say 'It's all right. Please don't cry. I'm trying to help. You can't go on like this.' And you get the parents absolutely screaming abuse at you: 'You fucking bitch! You're nothing but a ...' You know, the whole bit. Of course, it's all your fault.

But that wasn't the end of it. Shortly afterwards, I left Heidelberg and I went to other places. I heard that these children had only been in care for a matter of months before being given back to the parents, who were, in my opinion, not 'normal'. Not only did they get these children back; they had another one a few years later, and it died in a car on a forty-degree day – it had been left without ventilation for about ten or fifteen minutes. The child died from dehydration. That demonstrated the level of these people's parenting skills. I don't remember what happened as a result but I know that it was dreadfully distressing. In my opinion, they should have been charged with manslaughter.

In the meantime, I happened to be working on the gate of the police exhibit at the Royal Melbourne Show and they came out to the Show. When they came through, they recognised me and I recognised them. I have never seen people move as quickly as they did, with two kids in tow; and, in the pram, the third one who would be dead just months later.

'Were they contrite over the death?'

No, what was there to be contrite about? That's just life. You know, that's the way it is. (*Her expressive face demonstrates the sheerest futility as she shrugs.*)

I think a lot of police, if they are honest, have strong views on this subject – it gets very hard. The point is that you know full well that anybody who lives like that can't be the full quid – no sense of responsibility, no parenting skills, that sort of thing. I know it's controversial to say something like this but, because of what police get to see, we all feel that there are some people who should never be allowed to have children. And that particular family was a case in point. They should *never* have been allowed to have two, let alone the third.

A lot of so-called intellectually disabled kids can be very productive members of society. I had a very good friend, who had four children, three of them intellectually impaired. The first one was the worst and they didn't realise back then that there was a blood incompatibility between the parents. But it's to these parents' credit that their boys are now all very involved members of society. There is a difference where you've got an intelligent parent who has had a misfortune and a defective birth, and has made the most of it. But it would be a very sad thing if any of those children were allowed to have children themselves, because the condition could be hereditary.

A woman had picked up the phone and dialled 000 as her de facto was holding back her head and cutting her throat. Moments later, another phone rang and a little boy was saying, 'Can you please come and help? My mummy's boyfriend is hurting her.'

I used to work at D24 and this can expose you to a lot of trauma. But one incident distressed me more than any other. The D24 operators took an emergency call and all we heard was this gurgling scream. All my life I had known that there was terror, that people could express terror and be fearful and afraid. I had seen it, eyes wide; heard it with my own ears. But until this, I did not know there were *degrees* of terror, and you could hear it in this gurgling scream. A woman had picked up the phone and dialled 000 as her de facto was holding back her head and cutting her throat. Moments later, another phone rang and a little boy was saying, 'Can you please come and help? My mummy's boyfriend is hurting her.' He killed her – he cut her throat and she died. Just as the gurgle was starting to fade away, the phone was hung up. Now that was thirteen years ago, yet it has haunted me. I can close my eyes and hear it still. And it's the most horrible thing I've ever heard.

The cop who took the call was sitting there so helpless – in those days we didn't have the buttons that you can now press to trace the call, so as to get somebody to rescue them. And to find out later that you were sitting there listening to somebody dying, it was just awful. He was very good – he ended up on the phone with the little kid and he was saying 'Everything is going to be all right. Where are you?' The kid saw a petrol station and he said 'I'm near a petrol station.' The D24 operator told the boy to go to the petrol station and the police would come and meet him there. He handled it very, very well.

Nowadays everybody who goes through an incident like that has the facilities to go and talk it through, to get counselling, grief counselling, whatever they need.

Our lamb turns up, with a pot each of lovely innocent lemon squash. And Colleen continues ...

The policeman who was on the radio panel the night of the Hoddle Street shootings – top bloke, good ex-detective – had gone on to D24 to get his promotion, went back, did his time and then got back to the CIB. We had a lot of time for each other. I was working with him one night ages afterwards and I asked him how he thought he had coped after Hoddle Street. 'Oh, it didn't bother me at all,' he said fairly convincingly. Not long after the conversation, a job came down the chute involving shots that had been fired in Clifton Hill near Hoddle Street. This 'unaffected' man went to pieces for some seconds. He held the job card in his hand and said 'Shit, shit, not again!' He recovered quickly and handled the call very professionally. But he, too, should have had some counselling after Hoddle Street, since by then it *was* available. I don't know whether he did, but I believe he's out of the job now.

One gulp of breath …

I also knew one of the policewomen who was working on the night of the massacre. She was keeping the white board log of events. Everyone on duty was wearing headsets and you were all linked and the policewoman was writing up the details on the white board – who was where, who was doing what – so the operator could glance to see what was going on. Anyway, one of the units came up and said '203 [or whatever he was]. I have just been shot.' And the policewoman just kept writing – it was her husband and of course she recognised his voice. She just went into overdrive and kept going until somebody twigged and got there. Fortunately it was only a grazing wound, but as she kept working, my God, she didn't know how badly he'd been shot.

'What about the physical equipment you need for the job? I guess when you are young, the desire to keep the community in check is limitless, so the energy is boundless, and you were appointed for physical strength. But can you recall a time, later in your career perhaps, when you weren't up to it?'

That's the trap that police can fall into, that they put on that blue suit and they are invincible. That means there can never be an energy drop for a second. In reality, there is, but you think you can always overcome it because that little bit of blue material has 'magical powers' …

'… separates you from what's mortal.'

Sure. You're putting up with so much all the time, and although you can hardly drag yourself around, the energy seems to come from somewhere. When the F19 demos were on we'd get called out at 2 am, work sixteen hours, then go home. Then something would come up, and – bang – you'd do the ring-around to call everybody back, and you'd be on the job again. Police learn to sleep with their eyes open, while they're standing up. In those circumstances you eat as much as you can *when* you can because you don't know when the next meal will be.

But when you're under duress, there's really no separating physical and mental reserves. One policewoman who was a friend was involved in a situation where she and a police partner had the unenviable task of having to shoot burnt sheep, including lambs, after the 1985 bushfires. Afterwards she came around to my house so hyped, the adrenalin was rushing so much, that she didn't stop talking from the moment she walked in the door. I said 'Give me your car keys. You're not going anywhere.' And I went to bed that night thinking 'People should know about this. People should know that this is the sort of thing police do.' I guess that's where I tread a funny line, because I was away from the police force for four and a half years, in the real world being a so-called 'normal' person, and then came back to being 'police' at the age of twenty-eight, with a whole heap of insights.

A second gulp of breath ...

Colleagues would produce notes from courses they'd taken, but I had the life experience that they were too young to have. I have been through a divorce and all sorts of things that gave me an understanding of life. I really, truly believe that the minimum joining age for police should be twenty-five because people do need life experience. You can quote me, and I'll get into trouble for it, but kids barely with bum fluff on their chin go into a domestic situation involving somebody like you or me, with our grey hairs and so on, and they stand there quite seriously and say 'Now you've got to do this' and the other person of course is going to say 'How the hell would you know?'

I mean, there are good rookies and there are bad rookies. One really good rookie, I got to know one night when he and I went out to a car that had run into a tram in Plenty Road, Preston. It was chaos, absolute chaos. We were first on the scene and likely to be the only ones there because everyone was busy. I got out of the car and I was saying 'You do this, you do that, and I want you to go and ...' Just organised the whole thing, got traffic flowing, got the ambulances through, did what had to be done, cleaned it all up and left.

And this young copper, a little bit down the track, said 'How did you do that?' I said 'Do what?' 'How did you know what to do?' and I said 'It's just experience.' People look to the police to do that sort of thing, so you do it. And it's just astonishing what you *can* do, just by using your head – even off duty.

I remember, once, there was a baby choking in a supermarket and the people with it didn't know what to do. I went up and said 'Can I help?' It was a very, very hot day and I just picked up the child and put it on a glass-top counter. The shock of the glass got the wind going and the baby was fine, which was fortunate. Everyone said 'Oh, wow. How'd you do that?'

The emotions are there always – always. What you do is suppress them and deal with them another time. But it's the coppers who suppress them and never deal with them who end up in trouble, who end up with burnout, who end up with post-traumatic stress disorder.

'Just common sense.'

Yes, but helped by the training that you have to disassociate yourself from your emotions. The emotions are there always – always. What you do is suppress them and deal with them another time. But it's the coppers who suppress them and *never* deal with them who end up in trouble, who end up with burnout, who end up with post-traumatic stress disorder. Even now, and I've been retired seven years, I know that if I got talking about some things, it would become overwhelming for me. You've also got to be able to admit that you're human and that you are subject to those sorts of feelings.

'What are the signs of exhaustion?'

Your judgment becomes fuzzy. 'I'm all right, Jack. I can do this, I can do that. I'm foolproof.' You're not, of course: you're human. You are a person first. You probably recognise exhaustion less in yourself than you do in other people.

'Can you describe any achievements that you regard as a triumph?'

Yes, the Heidelberg rapes case – 1977. A series of rapes were uncovered, which became known as the Heidelberg rapes – you would have read about it in the newspapers. A small team of policewomen was formed. The first girls I dealt with had heard about Betty Blockbuster Follies and the catchphrase 'Ullo Schveetie', which I used a bit at the time. I guess the victims thought I was 'with it' and found me easy to talk to. The offenders' solicitors somehow heard that I had been using the phrase and thought I was trivialising the events that had taken place. It was thrown up at me at the committals. I was standing behind the girls while they were in the witness box. When one of the girls was testifying, there was this barrage from a line-up of about eight or nine solicitors. One of them said 'We have been told that policewoman Woolley was making light of what happened. She was joking with you and you were making fun of everything.'

My heart sank. I thought the case was going to be thrown out right then and there. At sixteen this girl had been brutalised by these men in ways you wouldn't believe and she just turned to him and said 'No, she didn't. She realised that what we had been through was just so horrible, all she was trying to do was make us feel better.' Why I didn't jump up and hug her then I'll never know. And I thought 'Where did that bit of wisdom come from?' You know, it was just so good.

But as a result of that I was banned from the rest of the committal hearing. I had achieved such a rapport with the girls. All I would say to them was 'Look, you tell the truth because as long as you tell the truth no one can harm you.' As the years went by – and it was some years before various things got to trial, it was so fragmented – the girls had grown up. They were fifteen and sixteen when a lot of these offences were heard. We interviewed 83 complainants and witnesses; we arrested and charged 15 blokes with 225 offences; and among those offences, there was one, a common law offence dating back centuries, whereby a person commits 'acts so terrible as to cause horror to diverse of her majesty's subjects' and really that was the best way you could describe it because there was nothing in law to cover the unspeakable things these guys had done.

Eight or nine policewomen worked sixteen hours a day taking statements from the complainants and witnesses. The evidence started stacking up – forensic evidence and all the other evidence – that this had all really happened. I believed so strongly in these girls but I was so junior in the policing context that I had to keep my mouth shut. I wasn't in the CIB, just seconded to the CIB. Some of the hardened senior detectives didn't believe that the events had happened but it was the forensic evidence that vindicated the girls.

'How did you obtain the convictions?'

We did dawn raids and got the evidence and identified the prime suspects that we wanted. They had heard that we were investigating and that the police were working in secret from what was then a disused police establishment. We got word that they were going to try and get us and we took different routes home every night. It was a little bit worrying, especially as sometimes there'd only be two of you working at 3 am.

Come the day of the arrests, as soon as the sun was up, bang – we went out. We wanted to get eight of them all at once, keep them separate and not give them a chance to talk to one another. We particularly wanted this one guy, who didn't have any priors at all. I was body-wired and my superiors said 'All right, just turn on your tape as you walk up the driveway and keep it going. Make sure you project your voice so that you can keep a conversation going.'

I had the microphone tucked into my bra and the recorder tucked down the back of my skirt. It was the first time I had ever been armed, so I was a bit wary. As instructed, I switched on the tape as we were going up the gravel driveway. On the tape, you hear the gravel crunching and suddenly there's this *kaboom, kaboom, kaboom* – my heart pounding so hard on the tape that it almost wiped out the conversation.

In the suspect's room we found copies of contracts that the girls had told us about. I'd got one of the girls to draw up one of these contracts for me when we were taking the rape statements. And, blow me down if we didn't find exactly the same thing in this guy's room. The boys had drawn up contracts declaring that 'on this day in 1976 or 77, this undertaking is made between ... [and they had scribbled names like Mickey Mouse or Donald Duck – this sort of thing] and 'Mary Smith' that if she ever talks to the police or her parents or anybody about what has happened today we can come around and bash her up and torture her and trash her home' and this sort of thing. They were picking up really young girls and getting them to sign these contracts. When

I found one of them in this guy's room I felt over the moon. Gotcha!

And there were other things, too, such as a particular set of earrings that a girl had been wearing on the night when the boys, having gang-raped her, lined her up to see how hard you could hit a girl before she would fall down or pass out. The girl's parents had gone out for the night so the boys came around and the crime took place in a kids' rumpus room at the back of the girl's house. In the process of punching her in the face they not only broke her jaw but also opened up a bit of a cut. She was wearing an earring which had feathers on it. Later, blood was found on the feathers and we got that and tied it in as evidence. We also tied in hospital records – she had to go to hospital – and they concocted a story that they had rescued her from a gang of skinheads and taken her to hospital for help.

'So she was raped while she was still conscious?'

Yes, they sodomised her as well. And they knew she was terrified of insects so they said that they were going to put a beetle into her vagina. They had her on all fours and were discussing what they were going to do to her so that they could have a bit more fun. They had an electric drill, which they turned on and threatened to put up her anus to see whether it would take it.

This was a classic example of rape by fear. After she was taken to hospital later that night, the story got around the area about what had happened to her. The girls were their own worst enemies because the boys would go and pick another girl up off the street and say, 'You heard what happened to 'Mary'. You heard we let a swarm of bees loose in her vagina. You heard that we ripped out her bum with an electric drill. And we'll do the same to you if you don't do what we tell you.' And the girls would just say 'Do whatever you want.'

These 18- to 20-year-old boys from middle-class families in Ivanhoe, Watsonia, Heidelberg were all eventually caught, by a team of forty detectives, of which I was a member. They were all charged with multiple offences, involving different girls, and each trial was fragmented. So we had to go over the whole story time after time after time. What also made it difficult was that the girls couldn't give hearsay evidence – 'I heard what happened to 'Mary', I heard they put bees inside her' – that evidence couldn't be led when the trials were fragmented. At one stage there was even talk about taking over the Melbourne Town Hall for months to run the trial there, so that all the people who needed to be present could fit.

Anyway, one of the principal offenders who was charged with another offender, said part way through one of the trials, 'I wish to make a statement. I want to change my plea to guilty. I've been thinking about what happened. I was treating girls just like so many lumps of meat and I'm sorry' and the trial was aborted. He was sentenced and the other guy was retried on his own. But this went on for years and years.

And in the end the girls just couldn't cope with it any more. One girl was examined by her doctor who said 'If I didn't know you better, I would say that you were suffering severe malnutrition and were heavily into drugs', because her teeth started to fall out, and it was the sheer stress.

Even as police, you should never, not ever, lose your ability to be appalled. Any police officer who goes through a stage where they are totally unshockable should get out.

'Have you any real understanding why these sorts of crimes occur or is it just a mystery?'

Actually that's a very interesting point. The public says 'Gee, that's terrible, that's horrible. How could people do such a wicked thing?' But if it doesn't come within the ambit of their own experience, they don't comprehend the horror of a lot this stuff. Even as police, you should never, not ever, lose your ability to be appalled. Any police officer who goes through a stage where they are totally unshockable should get out. I am not saying be overly emotional, but I am saying acknowledge the fact that there are still things that are very brutal and very shocking.

The cruelty in any person, I think, has a capacity to be limitless, if it's not controlled and if that control doesn't come at a very early age. Parents need to be saying to their children things like 'This is a very lovely little caterpillar, this is a lovely little butterfly, so don't pull its wings off. All right?' Because it is surprisingly true that kids who pull wings off flies turn out to be horrible people.

On the subject of people being immune to horror, I had occasion to talk, thirty years down the track, to the woman who had been the victim of the much-publicised three-year-old child rape case. She had reached the age where she wanted to know what happened and, particularly, she wanted to know what happened to the offender. She wanted to try and understand why he had done these things to her and I helped her looked up some of the information.

Anyway, this former three-year-old and I went to the library together and we looked up everything about what had happened to her and we read the newspapers of the trials and all this sort of thing. We were talking about how the public doesn't understand the horror. I was sitting alongside of her, reading articles, and she said, 'The poor little thing!' She was talking about someone else, not herself. It really moved me and I thought 'The former self is what she's looking at.' And I also thought 'Yes, it is so horrible that she can't equate it to herself and I hope she never does.'

'Did she go on to have children, bear children?'

She had major reconstruction and they said she would never be able to have children. But she had three. She turned out to be a lovely woman.

That experience of following through must have felt heartening for you.'

It was nice, it was great. I have the knowledge and the contacts. And I was able to track down, and tell her, the news that the perpetrator was now dead, so she could put it all to rest.

I forgive people but I never forget.

'Were there any criminals in your earlier working history whom you found you couldn't forgive? Does that ever crop up – that you can't find it in your heart to forgive, or consider them beyond forgiveness?'

No. For my own peace of mind, I forgive people but I never forget – an important distinction. I forgive them because who the hell am I to sit in judgment, you know? What right have I got to be that judgmental? I've got things in my life that I don't want people to be judgmental about. So it should work both ways.

Rather than 'unforgivable', a better word for some people's behaviour is 'incomprehensible'. In the Heidelberg rapes, two particular guys who had committed those acts of horror really were horrible people. I couldn't bring myself to speak to them at the time.

'In amongst all the gloom, you must have experienced some lighter moments ... At least I would hope you did!'

I'll tell you about some funny incidents from long ago. When I was working on the 000 switchboard, you'd get the nut calls and you'd get the heavy breathers and all that sort of thing. If they knew there was a policewoman on – and you were on for an hour at a time – you'd get a string of calls from these people. There was one policewoman there, who happened to be married. The rest of us, working the afternoon shift one day, heard her say, 'No thanks. I've already had one this morning'. Then she disconnected the caller. He rang back and said 'Have you really?'

I had a kid ring one day: 'You'd better get the fire brigade and the police and everyone here real fast because there is a big fire at the footy ground.' I could hear other kids in the background and I knew it was a hoax. So I said 'Now, are you telling me truth?' and he said, 'Yeah, yeah, yeah. You'd better get 'em here real quick, with their sirens on and everything.' I said 'OK. Now, have you got an adult with you?' Mutter, mutter, mutter in the background. 'Yeah, hang on a minute.' Next thing this little voice comes back on the phone, 'Hello, this is my uncle speaking.'

The naivety of children! And what about that lovely story you mentioned about addressing the kids from Broadmeadows.'

You get a group of kids in an area who cause trouble and it tends to reflect on the rest. While Broadmeadows was certainly a repressed area at the time, there were a lot of good kids out there and there were a lot of good things happening. But some of the kids would get really tough and come on with, you know, 'I can fix you', 'I'll be waiting for you', and all this bravado stuff. It can get threatening. I just pretended I didn't care, and said: 'Look, you don't worry me, I've had my throat cut and I'm still here talking to you, so don't try to make those threats because they won't work.' And they immediately backed off. This was one occasion when I was on my own, without a radio, and there was a large group that was really threatening

You know, a surgeon had cut my throat. *They* didn't know that's what it meant and there was this sort of backhanded respect for the fact. So it was something very handy that I was able to use – and I have used it more than once.

'When you have to question children, do you use a different method from the one you use to question adults? You know, adolescents whom you'd suspect of some misdemeanour?'

At sixteen or seventeen these days they know it all. Mostly, I just try to tough it out with them. I remember one kid of about fifteen, sixteen, who went around with some mates and together they got into vandalism and stuff. We took them back to the police station and separated them. This boy's parents came in, and they were the loveliest people. The mother was dying of cancer – she had literally months to go. The father had given up work to look after his wife. And away from these other little smart mouths, this boy was a lovely kid.

We had one of the complainants tell us that certain threats had been called out and one of the boys said 'Shut up you old fart. We're going to throw a bomb through your window.' When the allegation was put to him, this boy piped up and said 'Oh yeah, that was me.' He just said it straight away and I thought 'Oh shit, what'll I do?' These were the days before tape-recorders, when we actually had to make decisions about what should be recorded as the substance of the statement – you couldn't get down every single word. So I looked at the walls and windows and I said 'There are going to be charges that will have to come up to the Children's Court and if there were people who promised that they would never do anything like that again ...' I'm having this whole conversation out loud to myself, not looking at any of them '... Now I think I need to rephrase that question: Did you hear anybody call out some sort of threat?' He said 'Yeah, I did hear it' and I didn't take it any further. And he never came on notice again. I know, because I was at that particular station for a long time.

Interrogating people of any age is just a question of investigation. You are trained to be an investigator. You get your facts right, you then gather all the evidence and based on that you put facts to people. If you've got your facts right, half the time it's as simple as 'Oh yeah, you've got me.' All right, the real smarties today often don't succumb to this. But since I retired I've been an independent witness, which means I go to police stations and sit in on interviews with juveniles and I am far enough removed from my police work now to be able to divorce myself.

So there was this one boy, he'd come up from the country and the detective had come up from the country. I asked what the situation was and he told me there were assaults, burglary and all sorts of things. The detective said 'We've interviewed this kid hundreds of times and he's very well known. He's got a docket that thick – he's a real little shit.' And when they asked him the questions he would sit there and he would go like that – [*she makes a rude gesture*] and that would be his response. Then they'd ask him another question and he would just go like that – [*she makes the gesture again*].

So I went in and said 'Hello, my name's Colleen' and I shook hands with him. 'Now I'm here to listen to the interview. I will be taking notes because if anything comes of this and there are problems down the track I may need to give evidence on your behalf, and I am prepared to do that. Is there anything you'd like? Would you like a drink?'

'No, they'll just probably spit it in first.'

'Now, if you would like a drink I will get them to bring it in and I will have the first sip and if they've spat into it, I'll get it. How's that?'

'Oh, no, I don't wanna drink.'

Then the police came in to talk to him and he described who had done what for whom and he confessed to everything – even drawing a picture of the assaults and where everybody was situated. Yes, so a lot of it is in the way you treat them and that comes through. There's no point sitting down and talking to a Frenchman in Swahili when both of you understand a third language entirely. You talk to them at their own level and sometimes that can get to be very, very funny and you have great difficulty controlling your laughter. But of course you can, you learn to speak the lingo.

And that's one of the other fantastic things about the police force: the way they can speak the lingo. You can start out in the morning talking to the winos in doorways – they have been there all night and are in a bad way, and you've got to do something with them. And by lunchtime you could be performing duty with the Governor. The gamut of the population that you deal with represents the diversity of the population itself. And you have to be able to respond.

One guy rang up D24 one day and said 'Oh, you'd better get around to [let's say] 23 Smith Street. I've just shot me mate.' Now the policeman who was taking the call was quick enough to give him a caution: 'You are not obliged to say or do anything, but anything you do say may be given as evidence, do you understand that?' He said he did. And the policeman said, 'Where are you? And what just happened?' And he repeated it, and *Bingo!* there's the confession.

There seems to be a perception that young people coming into the police force are not going to make a lifetime career of it. Why on earth not?

'If you could analyse dedication, in the same way that scientists look at radioactive filament, what would you say dedication is composed of?'

I find it very worrying – and please publish this – that there seems to be a perception that young people coming into the police force are not going to make a lifetime career of it. Why on earth not? I mean, I would be in the police force now were it not for my injury. I loved it and it was very much like a vocation. But there seems to be a perception that you won't be here too long. But doctors don't go into doctoring so that they can go off and be bricklayers. I wanted to be a policewoman before I knew what a policewoman was. My father was a fireman, four of his five brothers had been policemen and they didn't have 'lady fire-men' in those days. So I wanted to be a policewoman – so far as I can remember it's all I really wanted to do. You take an oath of office and if it's something you have been thinking that you really, really want to do. It's a sacred oath really.

'What was your guiding principle in taking that oath?'

That maybe I could make a difference. And I was lucky enough – and it happened only once – that I had feedback. There was a young girl who was causing all sorts of problems at home. My colleagues and I talked to her and talked to her, and I even remember her name, which is unusual with the hundreds of people you deal with. Then, one night, we went around to check on her because her father had contacted us to say 'We are going away. Mary's going to be home. Please ... there's been so much trouble.' So we go past, and all the lights are on and she's having a boozy party – probably just boozy, back then, and not druggy, although there may have been a bit of marijuana.

Now I knew that we wouldn't have a leg to stand on, but we closed the party down, took her in and locked her up for the night. We put her on a Protection Application and I knew damn well that that would either make or break her.

I was very cross because her father bailed her the next morning, instead of leaving her there until at least after lunchtime. But she had suffered the indignity of having to go in, be strip searched, be washed, the whole demeaning thing. She had to go to court the following day, and I said to her in court 'This is where you are headed. Winbirra [Remand Centre] was just the start. It's in your hands.'

The case was thrown out – I knew it would be because there wasn't enough to pin on her, but I wanted her to get a taste of what was coming. Years later, I rang my insurance company about something. Chat, chat, chat, and the woman helping me said, 'Excuse me, are you a policewoman? Do you remember me? I'm Mary.'

I said 'Yes, I do remember you.'

'I am so glad to talk to you. I want to thank you for what you did that night. I know now why you did what you did. I really had a look at myself. I've been in this job now for about four years. I'm getting promoted next week to head of my section. I'm engaged to be married and my life is fantastic. I get on so well with my parents.'

Now that was a dream come true! That one story kept me going and will keep me going. That I was able to make a difference in one person's life. It's so rare to get feedback.

'Did you have people writing letters of gratitude?'

Oh yes, I've still got copies of them. They're very precious to me because whenever I feel down, I just pull them out and think 'Oh well, I did something nice once.'

Some little kids would just come up and hold your hand and look at you with such trusting eyes. I was talking to a group of kids at a school and they were all fighting over who could hold your hand when you went from classroom to classroom or whatever. This particular day I only had a few minutes between classes. We were visiting every level but the staff toilets were way over the other side of the school so you had to use the kids' toilets. They were all hanging off me, so I go into this toilet and am sitting there with my knees around my ears. That's when I realised I had an audience, all going 'Shh, shh. Listen, listen. Ohhh, she did it!.' And afterwards they looked at me as if I was human: I 'did wees' at the toilet! They were just gorgeous.

'At the last Victorian election a lot of people complained that they didn't really know their Labor or Liberal members – they hadn't had any contact with them. Do you think that applies equally to the police, that the public feels they can't go to the police and talk to them?'

Some members of the public do and some don't and that will always be the way. I recently heard Chief Inspector Rod Norman from the Youth Advisory Unit talking about the turnaround they've got in the way they deal with kids now. They've got recruits at the Academy going out to this high-challenge course, working with kids who are in danger of getting into trouble, and developing a rapport with them. I thought 'What a great idea.'

It is a generation thing. It's going to take time. Ultimately if you have this sort of thing at grass roots level, your police force is going to become mainly a PR thing – ultimately, in generations to come. It will take a very long time because there are a lot of people to get to. But it's turned around from the old 'Give 'em a kick up the slacks and send them home' to what it is now. Policing and the community are both in a constant state of flux and the development of technology contributes to that. Our entire lifestyle contributes to that and it's up to every single person in the broader community – police and public alike – to adapt and grow with it.

There seems to be much better communication and much better rapport between the public and the police than there was in the 1960s and 70s.'

I get very, very cross with civil libertarians who go on and on and on about the rights of the crooks, not about the victims. I get so cross and what I did hear on Saturday at a seminar was a thing they're trialing down south with kids in conference situations – you know, the 'meet the victim' program. Children's Court senior magistrate Jennifer Coates was telling a story about one lad who, with some of his mates, had broken into an old guy's flat and the old guy was just hanging on to his independence. They threw his doona over his head and threatened to do all sorts of things to him if he didn't behave himself, and left. They were ultimately caught, but because this guy was just hanging on to his independence, that incident was enough to make him totally vulnerable. He became very frail overnight and was put into a nursing home. Six weeks later he died.

When this kid turns up to this conference, he finds out that the guy has died and he was so absolutely shattered by this, you know. He had no idea that silly bravado and thoughtlessness could lead to that sort of consequence and *he* sentenced *himself* to twelve months every Saturday, going and working at that nursing home. The solicitor tried to tell the moderator, 'Well I know you wouldn't impose a sentence that harsh, it doesn't warrant that because the death wasn't directly related to the incident.' Arguably, but the kid was adamant that that's what he wanted to do to make up for it. With that sort of thing happening, with the recognition that along with the person's rights there are inherent *responsibilities*, when we get that balance, then we're going to have a fantastic society to live in.

'When you look back on your career, could there have been any working life other than policing?'

No, not for me there couldn't. That's why I am glad I'm still involved with the Retired Police Association. Every single police officer I'm involved with has hopeful stories, funny ones and sad ones.

'Well, it's good that we can give the public a chance to read some of yours, at least. In a sense, these are their own stories.'

Absolutely. Without their half of it, there wouldn't *be* a story.

Fred Silvester

Emigrated from England as police constable 1949

Joined Victoria Police 1949

Retired as chief inspector 1983

Crims fly Concorde; cops walk

Fred Silvester

In Dolby stereo at Fred Silvester's beach resort at Loch Sport, down in winter Gippsland, The Three Tenors are giving a booming concert performance tonight. Boy, is the music loud! Can't see a thing here, except an old Pom copper in the half-dark. It's so dark there's only the video gleam on his jug ears as he sinks down into the easychair to enjoy the deafening delivery of Pavarotti and his musical mates. Fred's wife June screams over the music that dinner is ready. 'D'ya want it cold?'

Fred sips a beer and mutters something discernible only as mockery.

Nicknamed 'The Cat' by the police-fearing community in Melbourne for his uncanny ability to shinny both up and down gas pipes at speed, Mr Silvester used to breathe in lots of suffocating plaster vapour and silicone dust when he dropped in on illegal gaming, particularly during one of his infamous SP bookie raids. He was once the most feared copper in Australia – or 'the most hated', as he puts it, sinking ever lower into the womb easychair. We have dinner, which is succulent vegetables adorned with a rather marvellous cheesy sauce that Mrs Silvester has just made, and lovely drooly chicken, and converse.

'My memory's had the Richard', he confesses, but June holds his hands across the dining-room table and sings to him. This is a new experience for me: I've never heard a wife sing to her husband before, let alone 'a policeman's missus', as Fred calls her.

June Silvester's voice is extremely melodic. Her voice is his favourite melody and he looks down a bit but beams. Fred spears a lump of broccoli and grumbles. 'Oh, well, we'll see how the memory works in the morning.' They're putting me up for the night, on the understanding that the interview will be in the morning over breakfast.

I listened to the Gippsland wind belt up the roof all night until at last I fell asleep downstairs in the spare bedroom, having

112

drifted into unconsciousness watching Essendon flay Carlton. In the morning I heard the old policeman stuffing round with eggs and coffee and so on. 'Scrambled eggs?' he crooned.

Down at the Loch Sport shops, where we went to pick up the Sunday paper, a friend of Fred's was waiting in the freezing cold for the milk bar to open. He swore and blasphemed more than any other man I've ever met. Inside, there were people, yet we just hung around outside for about an hour. How about opening up? I thought. It's not like that in the bush, is it?

I enjoy the cold, but this air appears frozen. There was a chill factor 15 on the tired old wind-tortured public seat where Fred sat with his mate. 'It's a cunt, that fuckiin' wind; a cunt,' the man muttered.

To which Fred added 'It is a cunt', and they looked together at nothing.

They swore all the time, the two mates, mostly the swearing had to do with the weather, but as I wandered away to the Antarctic-type foreshore or lake, for it was difficult to learn whether it was lake or ocean or loch, I head them swearing about rates and cost of living.

When we got back to Fred's, as we crossed his threshold, I asked him the difference between cops and crims.

'Crims fly Concorde; cops walk.'

He looks like he's had a deep sleep and is set to bust. 'Jesus,' he curses as he sits across the kitchen table with his hands folded round the percolator and favourite cup. His ears in the early morning light catch a finger of biscuity sunshine. His thick grey curly hair stands up, surprised-looking. He's pretty bald, but the eyes are so alive and he looks straight through you, eyes full of humour. His voice is still very Englishy, with an Australian ringbark undercut. It is a chippy voice, unhesitant, and straight to the truth it goes. He came to Australia in the late 1940s, having worked as a London Metropolitan Policeman, or 'Bobby' as they were known.

When I was stationed at Wang, I learnt more about policing then anywhere else I ever went, and that includes the States, New York, Vancouver, whatever. There were some terrible people at Wang. Oh, there are good and bad everywhere. That goes without saying, you know. For instance, there was this magistrate. He took children who were wards of the state from the watch-house to his home to do what he liked with them.

Fred shrugs his shoulders in their big woolly track top, as if to say 'What can I do?'

He just asked the watch-house keeper to release the boy in his custody for a few hours. He should not have done it, but he was a magistrate, let's face it. Well, that didn't have complaints, by the way. And there was no evidence that he touched them, or even made any suggestions.

'No, no, it's just hearsay, isn't it?'

It's just the fact that he took them out. But anyway – he is no longer a magistrate. And I believe he's dead. Now I hope he is.

This happened a long time ago, but he's still incensed – a fanatic for justice.

You had to do everything in Wang, and everything was the daily requirement of coppers in Wang – from railway ticket evasion to murder, all in the one hour or day. Everything was on your neck.

Kids, kids, kids, *he says, hopscotching subjects, back to the mid-fifties in Wangarratta.* Kids with this morning bright sun in their eyes and a drunk driver cleaned them up. Straight through them. This happened out the back of Wang. When I got there, I said 'Who's the driver?' This bloody bloke slurred his words. I said to my partner Frank, 'Look. You take all the particulars here. I'll deal with this bloke.' I had to go to about three doctors before I could get one to examine him. They just didn't want to get involved. Anyway, I got one doctor who said, 'Yeah, he's drunk.' So I locked him up. In fact, I charged him with manslaughter.

And both the coroner and the detective said 'You'll never get a conviction on manslaughter, particularly in the country here.' Anyway, Jocky, the magistrate, he committed him for trial at the coronial inquiry, because the magistrate was also the coroner. And he was convicted. He got six months.

That would have been something of a triumph in those days, wouldn't it? A conviction like that, with all the trouble to prove drunkenness before breathalysers came in.'

As far as I know, that was the first conviction for manslaughter by motor car.

'Did he show remorse?'

No. He couldn't have cared less. He laughed and joked about it on his way to court. Well, you never know what people are really thinking. He might have been just putting on a big act.

Fred's head is in his hands and he's rubbing his bristly brow.

How did I feel about him? What's that matter? You keep a lid on it. Go to the pub. Drink with your mates. Your fellow coppers.

He shields his craggy eyes from the morning sun, partly because it's annoying him and partly because he is seeing the incident again.

You got no overtime. No one knows how hard you worked. No one.

Now he is speaking of the long hours studying Victoria police official work diary, a record of rostered hours from 1951 to 1955 when he was at Wang. He puts on his glasses. June sleepily wanders in and loudly stacks last night's plates in the sink. 'I do,' she yells, and goes and turns on a computerised poker game, and sits to compete with it. Fred looks up at her.

You wouldn't have a clue. Look here. 385 hours cold. You got no time off. (*He pounds his index finger into the duty book to show June those hours of long ago.*) 380 sick days behind, I was, when I left the force. The sick leave, it accrues. If you do become sick, you use your credits. But if you don't become sick, you don't use your sick credits and they're forfeited.

An old copper going over his old knocked-off hours, faithfully hand-lettered in a battered notebook in a neat hand. He looks up at me as if to say, 'What are you doing here?' I ask him about his first feel of a gun. 'How'd that feel?'

I pulled a pistol in Wang once, but it was too full of tobacco to go off. It'd been hanging round in a drawer too long. How did I feel at the time? Well, I thought at the time, 'What's the good of this?'

We used to be the unpaid counsellors. Nowadays, coppers want professional counsellors, or trauma bullshit.

He scrapes his bristly chin and sips his coffee, daintily. He jumps up now restless and paces around in a fury. His voice is up a notch. Terribly restless.

We used to be the counsellors. We were the unpaid counsellors. I remember screaming at a priest who wanted me to help him out with a deceased man at Wang Base Hospital. The man had died in a motorcar accident and the clergyman wanted me to tell the parents. And I replied, 'That's your job, isn't it?' Nowadays, coppers want professional counsellors, or trauma bullshit. We were the unpaid counsellors in those days. You went into it, everything I mean, and just did your job, as long as you could.

There was corruption everywhere, everywhere I tell you. You look at the *Herald* Wealth Words crosswords competition. Do you remember that? There was this Justice Stark. He defended the Herald and Weekly Times against my charges that it was illegal gaming. So I sought permission to re-interview their editor at the *Herald* and he said, 'I've got nothing to say.' Now, I don't know if you're familiar with the crossword puzzle called Wealth Words, but it was terribly popular in the '60s and it was big money if you won. Really big money – eighty thousand, ninety thousand, pounds. There was already a solution and most of the clues had two, three, four or five alternatives that would fit the clue, so of course it was sheer luck whether you picked the right one or not. So you had to do about twenty-five to thirty of them for any hope of a win. That was a lottery all right.

The way around this was for them to get a permit. They've all got bloody permits! I prosecuted that case myself, and Stark defended it. He won it for the Herald group, and they kept the puzzle going.

'Do you have any regrets?'

I regret very much not taking that twenty thousand quid a week to turn a blind eye to a perfectly respectable starting price bookmaker. That is a very big regret. Those SP bookies I raided ... now, some of them were scum, and some of them were very intelligent and respectable businessmen.

Claps his hand over his forehead again theatrically.

I want to just about die when I think of all my hard slog, dropping through silicon ceilings and hiding in draughty roofs for days or hours on end to raid bookies, and then the former Kennett Government comes out openly courting gaming – promoting it – gaming at any costs was Kennett's motto. Don't forget there were commissions of enquiry into betting.

That sort of government has destroyed the country. Poker machines are ridiculous. These machines, with the government's endorsement, are destroying ordinary battlers. I was involved in a poker machine enquiry. That was a breakthrough a few years back. Now every pub has poker machines. I've wasted my life! Brothels were illegal. Not now. They, too, are encouraged by the government. Why did I raid all these illegal massage parlours? Why did I bother? I thought I was doing good. Not now, not any more.

He drifts now into a response to a query from me last night about today's need, in the fight against crime, for interpreter services. Fred's brow grows black, and he stands up, dramatically to make the point, grasping an imaginary criminal by the throat.

We never needed interpreters. All this different language bullshit. I just said, 'Right-O matey, where were you last night?' They understood 'last night'. Never mind the different language bullshit. I was speaking their language. If I went into a house in Toorak I wouldn't speak to the people like that. You spoke everyone's language. You've got to be able to speak as they do – all of them.

He sits and takes a breather. June points and clicks and smokes and stares. He says he retired in Canberra about fifteen years ago after a great deal of frustration over not being able to do that job as he wanted to.

I was an assistant commissioner, Victoria police, and I was the director of the Australian Bureau of Criminal Intelligence. I started it off. There were seven commissioners, and I only trusted one: my own commissioner. You look at Sir Terence Lewis. He was corrupt. And that was found out. I had to put up with him. I was supposed to report any criminal intelligence to *them*. I mean, come on! (*Glares at me, as if to say, 'What's the point?'*)

Back to Wang, where things made sense. The mention of the word Wang seems a respite or oasis.

At Wang, when I was there, we had to supply all sorts of things to incredibly ungrateful farmers; farmers take all day to get anything done. Anyway we had to put Motor Registration labels on their vehicles – you know, the gummy little things. As if we didn't have enough work to do, and you're unpaid anyway on bloody long weekends. Farmers are the worst kinds of people! (*Pounds the table.*) They've got you all Saturday afternoon for their fucking car stickers. You quickly realise it's not a working day in the city, is it? You never get a cent overtime. And all their superiority going on about what big farms they've got, showing you their stupid big cars, and me with no overtime on Sunday.

One day I had just got through handing out all their stupid stickers to them, and filling in all the paperwork, went back to the station in a stinking mood – absolutely worn out, I was. And there was this young man, sitting there. Apparently he'd been sitting there all day, waiting to see me at Wang. And I just snapped at him. I said, 'What do you want, mate?' And in a whisper he said, 'I've backed over my little son in the driveway, and I thought I should come here to say so.'

Fred's chin crumples in sympathy with the memory, the awful memory. And the grief of it has wiped the smile off his face. We sit for half a minute, just looking at each other. After all the comic stories and bad temper, he looks so different now and much older than an hour or so earlier when we started talking, when we walked back from the beach.

'Where are you from, Fred?'

I was born in Letchworth in Hertfordshire, England.

'Is that where you were when you got news of the war breaking out? Your mother must have got the news. Did she?'

Yes. I remember it clearly. My mother was sick at the time. We didn't have television back then, just a radio. It wasn't even called a radio. It was a wireless. I'm listening to the wireless there one night, listening to the news. 'The Admiral here regrets the loss of one of those ships, off the west coast of Africa ...', and my mother said, 'Your father was on that!' I said, 'Don't be silly.' And anyway he was. He survived. Just got wet. He saved his money, that's about all, because he had a money belt on. He was in the water for six hours before getting picked up.

'Let's go to the Blitz. You were there, weren't you, when the bombing was on in London. In the 1940s.'

Oh, yeah, we were in a war, though, don't forget, and we knew that every night. During the Blitz, our old home was only twenty-five miles from London and we were on the flight path.

'With the Blitz attacks, what was the sound of them?'

Well, the drone of the aircraft is what you heard for a start. Then the anti-aircraft fire ... and then later when they got the night fighters up, the machine-gun fire. There was the crunching of the bombs when they dropped. (*Coughs.*) And then all your windows broke. If they didn't hit your house. (*Coughs.*)

There was a nice girl next door, and she used to come around, and we used to sleep together under the table.

June's voice from the kitchen: 'That'd be right.'

'Were you a larrikin?'

According to all reports.

'How about your own report?'

I reckon I was an angel. I was a choirboy and all that sort of thing.

'Did you have a rebellious nature?'

Well, I was rebellious after my mother died. That's for sure. And I had a real hate against the world. About this time my father was sent back. My mother was dying. This is in '41. It was for her that he came home, and later on she died.

They tried to make me read Latin. I was trying to matriculate. I had lots of girlfriends, according to my sisters. Our teachers were tough and you didn't fool around with them. Masters and mistresses, it was, in our day. Grammar School. Mortarboard and tassel. Disciplinarian. I suppose you've seen the film *Goodbye Mr Chips*? It was like that. I had a couple of mates, and there was no home life after that. We were all farmed out.

I went into the Navy at seventeen. This is 1943 – a turning point in my life really. And I went back to a bit of discipline, which I suppose I needed. I got put through some commando courses, which I wasn't really rapt in, and I thought, 'I'm supposed to be an engineer in the Navy.' Got out in December '47. I had a few differences with my father but I patched them all up. I went home on leave; I had seventy pounds to spare. I had a cardboard attaché case make out of compressed cardboard.

There I was enjoying myself at home, feet up nice and cosy and that sort of thing, pretty relaxed, and the old man said to me, 'What do you think you're going to do for a living?' I could've had a mechanics job, no worries, and gone through my life doing that but I'd had enough of that sort of thing. I was trying hard to spend the seventy pounds.

But anyway, since he kept on at me about getting a job, I thought I'd better appease the old bugger and I picked up a paper one day, looked through Situations Vacant and I saw this London Metropolitan Police. So I thought, 'Ah, I'll apply for this.' Because I won't get this job, but at least I can tell him I applied.

Much to my considerable surprise and concern I got the job. Fitness test – passed that. Medical examination – passed that. A big bloke in front of me, and one behind me. I got through and they missed out. (*He shows a cockiness common to all little coppers. Little fearless ones, that is.*)

'So when did you join up exactly?'

Third of February '47. Twenty-first birthday was spent walking through the doors of Peel House. Big grey bluestone thing. Up in Islington. And I was sent to Hendon Police College.

He shows me a photograph of many London bobbies freezing together.

We were all posted out in the metropolitan area. We were the London bobbies. What do you learn? You learn law. Police procedures. All that sort of thing. You got the sack if you strayed. It was a three-month course. Two pound a week, plus accommodation at a station house. It was fun chasing barrow boys. There were bashings, street stalls on wheels, like barrows selling fruit and other stuff under the mat. They had to apply to hold a street permit, charges like obstructing traffic. It was a sea of apples and pears. Peas everywhere. Nylon stockings much sought after. Left there in '49. Came out here.

His arms are out, expansive, swinging his jar of coffee with a flourish to show distance.

I did particularly well there. Was sent on loan to the CIB as a Plain Clothes. Night shift on your own. Worked your beats. Waterloo Station. Prostitutes. They're still there in the West End. (*Said as though these are the same women, but he's joking.*)

> *Once I intercepted a barrow load of bananas and the thief couldn't explain to me where he got the bloody things from. Bananas were pretty rare in England at that time. And when he eventually told me, I went, 'Righto. You're nicked.'*

'Did you investigate any murders?'

There were a few murders. They were common enough. Once I intercepted a barrow load of bananas and the thief couldn't explain to me where he got the bloody things from. Bananas were pretty rare in England at that time. And when he eventually told me, I went, 'Righto. You're nicked.' Then I had to push the bloody bananas myself to hand them in, and they're perishable. The charging sergeant said, 'What are you going to do with those bananas?' I said, 'I don't know.' He said, 'Well you bloody well get rid of them.' So here I am wheeling stolen bananas around, offering them to hospitals. (*Laughs*)

'Is suspicion a part of good police work?'

You have to be on to everything and you must notice everything, instantly. There was this tinkle of glass once in Blackfriars Road.

I heard that tinkle and saw a thief's arm stuck in a window. Just stuck there. He was turning a lock to get in. That meant a lot so far as the evidence went, and I thought there must be some part of a thief's body in some part of the building.

I took notice of doors and locks. I noticed a bombed building, legacy of the Blitz. I noticed the padlock, a brass one, different from the lock that had been there an hour earlier. This is in the dark. On my beat. So I stood there with my ear to the door. I could hear voices inside. We broke in to the place and there were three blokes busily cutting down all the lead piping. That lead piping was worth a hundred pounds a ton. Caught them red-handed.

I'm unfailingly polite to criminals. On this occasion, I said, 'Good morning, gentlemen.' They were doing their job and I was doing mine.

'How do you address criminals when they're sprung?'

I'm unfailingly polite to them. On this occasion, I said, 'Good morning, gentlemen.' They were doing their job and I was doing mine. All they'd say was, 'Looks like you've got us this time.' Then you'd walk them. You might even have a natter about the cricket on the way, but only if we were winning. (England, that is.) And then the charge is read by the station sergeant.

'Did you work singly or in pairs as London bobbies?'

Well you're supposed to be in pairs, but at nights you couldn't do that because we didn't have enough of us. So we had all these police boxes and there was a telephone for public use that you could go inside, and inside it you could stay for a while. And you could view all around you, and you could have your lunch or whatever in it. You were supposed to be in a certain place at a certain time, which was something I objected to because I said, 'Look, if an inspector's supposed to know where I am, it's going to take a bloody crim less than a week to know where I am.'

'You would have had favourite streets, or favourite walks?'

Oh, yeah. Quite a lot of blokes had a favourite hideaway. One bloke used to get his sleep standing up. There's a story – I can't vouch for it – about one bloke who always used to do that, standing in the doorway, asleep, while the burglar was busy burgling the bloody building, while he was standing there. This bloke jumped out of the window with his bag or swag, right in front of the policeman and bloody woke him up.

He points to a photo of where he landed at Victoria Dock. Squints. Voice is gruffer for all the talking.

Got here September of '49, Melbourne that is. That's fifty years ago. Here are some of my mates from the intake. Here's George Stafford – he was senior constable, Victoria Police, who officially met us. On board the ship out here to Australia. Here's the training depot in St Kilda Road. When I first saw Melbourne I thought, Christ. Rusty iron roofs. Single storey bungalows. Melbourne looked like the end of the world. We went up the Yarra to 6 Victoria Dock. It's still there, too, where we disembarked.

'Full of hope?'

The truth of the matter is, I was going to use it as a holiday. I thought I'll stay a couple of years and then I'll go off somewhere else. The depot was all right. It was two squads combined with a few off another ship. We studied Social Science and we studied the geography of Victoria. I couldn't even find Victoria.

They'd ask you where Mildura was. What do they farm along the Goulburn? I've got a solution with exams. Generally speaking, no matter what your subject is, if you go back over say the last ten exams, you can nearly write the exam paper out for yourself, because the examiners seem to get themselves into a rut, and ask the same questions over and over.

He goes back to the intake photo again. He's breathing on the surface of the photograph and pointing at opaque faces.

He served his time out. Len Chapman. He served his time out. Fingerprints were his speciality. A police photographer. That bloke there has been here. He chased a rich widow to England and disappeared. That bloke there committed suicide. Jack Berwick there thought he was Mary, Queen of Scots.

His face zeroes in on the rookies. The forehead right on each. Quietly, he rattles off a roll call of deceased detectives:

He's dead. He's dead. He's dead. He's served his time. He's an Irish poet now for a living. He's moved from dog handling to Irish poetry. Paddy McGrath. (*The voice is disappointed, even crest-fallen.*) He used to be a dog trainer ...

I've always had publicity (*calling out to June*), haven't I darling? From the day I first arrived in Melbourne. As this picture of me testifies, when it was first published in the *Sun News Pictorial*. (*He flicks a binder of old yellowing cuttings to me and tells me his daughter is putting his life together but there are just so many stories.*)

There was so much corruption in gaming, and in the police force. So we set about wiping it out.

Here's a picture of an SP bookies' place in Shepparton. That was an early raid of mine. Two SPs had the place all tied up. It was a combined telephone and person-to-person. Back lane stuff. We were actually very busy in Melbourne. We were called Secret Seven. Mick Miller was sub-officer in charge. There was so much corruption in gaming, and in the police force. So we set about wiping it out. Let's talk about the Shepparton raid. There were slang words in those days. There was the Cockatoo, the look-out man. He sees cops coming. He's standing there in one of these panels, see? There was a contact behind it which flashed a light. It was a double fence. Part of it had a roof over it.

He's speeding. The voice is smooth like a train.

There was a little getaway passage and these little trip wires. So whatever you touched rang a bell. Why were the fines so low? Twenty-five dollars was the maximum penalty. If they were convicted a third time they went to prison. They got six months or more. False names. The magistrates knew their names were false. I can never remember one of them *ever* going to jail. That was the attitude of the courts. Ray Dunn defended 'em. Another magistrate, Old Tommy, he'd have his courthouse cleared by lunchtime so he could go and play golf. In the end I beat Ray Dunn, and I went to the Privy Council about it. That was a Baccarat case. It was Ray Dunn who actually gave me a legal opinion that Wealth Words *was* an illegal one.

He's reading through more albums.

You don't know what you'll find until you have a look. Here's a Licensing and Gaming Squad group photo, circa 1959, see? See Mick Miller? There's Mick, there. John Cook's dead. Bill Mackay died. Delacombe was Governor of Victoria. I'm wearing the Queen's Police Medal. Last time I wore a uniform. There's Father John Brosnan. Did I know him? Yes. He was the Catholic at

Pentridge. He was an extremely keen racegoer, frequently seen at the trots. He had the remarkable knack of being able to win remarkably often. Maybe he got help from up top.

He gets up and paces around again, sensing memories in backs of chairs and recollections in bookcases. He's restless. I'd say he's always been that way, but there's this calm too. And he loves to speak. A raconteur.

All my papers have been altered by some bastard.

'Probably you, love,' calls out June, boinking a poker sound in the corner.

I was posted to Russell Street first. That was my first stop. Here is my Beat Duty at Russell Street. (*Looks up at an old calendar. He remembers everything, all right. He's on a roll now.*) Sixth of March of '50, I went to Brunswick. Twenty-third of March of '51, I went to Camberwell. That was to do Beat Duty. Twenty-sixth of July '51, to Victoria Dock. On enquiry patrol and goods checking (*then gravely*) – things were being stolen. The dock itself used to disappear at night.

June laughs. I do also.

Cigarettes, fur coats, anything. Even a handful of nails. Charged over a handful of nails. I'd had enough! On the gates of the dock, that's where I was. It should never have been a bloody police job. Some things aren't on the invoice. It should show you the contents of what's there, of what you're supposed to check. I had a big blue over that. I was a constable still when I went to Wang.

There's a noticeable relief in the voice in the uttering of the fabled word Wang.

That was on the ninth of January '51. I went there and it was the best thing I ever did. In more ways than one.

He gazes up at all his citations and police awards from all over the world. Portraits of Fred in Honolulu and New York. He really has been from the bottom to the top. You can't get much higher.

I went to Wang because I just couldn't get a house in Melbourne. Country police stations often had houses with them. I was so cooped up and I wanted to go fishing in the country. Needed to get out the rod and have a go at the trout. I was married with one kid and no money. In Wang there were three or four houses set apart just for police. Three years I was in Wang. It was a 24-hour station. You did night duty, and on that you're on your own. There's no back-up. You copped it from murder down. You're not safe, even in the watch house. You've got to close up the watch house to deal with it.

One night, the copper who was supposed to relieve me was not there. In walks the milkman, and the milkman says, 'There's a lady up the lane, there. There's a lady in a nightdress. She fell.' So I wrapped some blankets around her and got the milkman to ring the ambulance. 'What's happened here?' I said to the fallen woman. 'I can't really remember,' she said, 'but I fell out of that window.'

He's frantically rubbing his chin now with the back of his hand. The voice is sandpapery.

And so she says to me, 'I'm tingling all over. Could you hold my hands please?' She landed on her knees. The ambulance finally came and she'd died. Of a broken neck. They turned her on her side in the hospital. (*His eyes show me they shouldn't have.*) That's never been solved, that case. She was bloody well pushed out of there. The bloody doctor that had been deregistered, he did it. (*Accusing.*) He did it! That was back in '52. (*His face shows that it is*

129

now, as well.) I believe she was pushed. The coroner brought down an open finding.

June, for some mystifying reason, switches the light off, plunging us all into profound darkness. I ask her if we can have it on again. June says, 'Oh, can't you see? It doesn't make any difference. Look.' I say 'Oh, it does, believe me.'

Now, look at that. This is a record of conduct and service. See what it says? It says, 'Silvester, Frederic Albert. Appointed Constable, 19/9/49.' So I went from Wang to CIB Detective in '55. Later in '55, I went to Carlton CIB. '56 back to Russell Street. It wasn't Section Duties but Gaming Duties. In '60 Company Fraud Squad. Promoted to Sergeant. Back to uniform. It's a bit hard to do that, actually. In '72 went to Operations Department as a co-ordinator of Special Groups. In Canberra I formed the Australian Bureau of Criminal Intelligence in '82.

'It seems like you've done everything that police can do.' And underneath the flippancy and all the joking and storytelling, I think to myself, the heart and soul of your endeavours has always been love of truth. Justice.

You're the first on the scene. You're supposed to contact the Homicide Squad if there's been a murder, so in a little country town like Wang, you've got to go and get him out of his bed. You know, you've got to wake him up first, and tell him what's what. Locals try to bribe you, and the bribery is expected to be accepted. Not with me, it isn't. It used to be customary for farmers to drop off spuds to the coppers' door. And there were eleven hotels in Wang – that's a lot of bloody drinking. And I couldn't be bought. Righto. Let's do the hours again.

And again picks up the little black duty books and squints at them. The nose collates the pages.

On Duty 8.30 am. Off Duty 7.30 am. That's nearly 24 hours! That was normal in those days. It's all here, in these books. This is what I really did. Saturday in Wang, here I was on duty at 8 am – till 11.30 pm. It's a remarkable roster. I had a young family. They never saw me. Not by the look of this. They didn't!

June sings out, 'You didn't work that long a shift.' Fred returns fire without a backward glance.

You wouldn't have a clue how long I worked. Nobody would.

He brightens. He seems refreshed, though he's been remembering for hours.

'Have you ever felt demoralised?'

He sits perfectly still. Makes himself sit stiller yet, before he can go into it. Good question, that one. Demoralised rather than frightened. I'm learning how to ask questions, as police have all their lives.

There was this bloke who committed suicide over 1200 pounds. He was an SP bookie. That demoralised me, I suppose.

Another time was at 100 Johnston Street, Collingwood. Something terrible had happened. We got the news. Got to get out there. Ernie Cartwright was my driver. We went flat to the boards. 'Car 100, there are two bodies.' A new car said three bodies.

By this time, there were four bodies, and not a firearm to be seen. It was done with a rifle. Each one had been shot seven times.

A single-shot .22 rifle. He had reloaded every time. He found out where his father was – in the bedroom, reading. He said, 'I've run out of matches, Dad. Have you got a match?' So when his dad reached over for a match, he blew him right between the eyes.

His stepmother tried to claw her way out of her room. Through the door, with her fingernails. But he broke the door down and put another seven bullets into her. He waited for his stepbrother and sisters to come home. He'd already taken the fuses out of the lights. You cut the fuse, you know. He told them the lights had fused. Then he shot him. He shot his stepbrother sitting in his car on the passenger side. This other woman in the car, she got out and ran for her bloody life.

The next night, he gave himself up. 'The policeman who was on last night, I want him,' he said, asking for me. So I got a call to go to Russell Street. Somebody wanted to see me in reception. It was him. He even started confessing everything there and then. So I took down all his statements, because later, I mean, he could have changed his mind. Later on he took me and showed me where he left one bullet on the window sill in Johnston Street, that he said he was going to use on himself, but he never did.

He had killed because he was sick and tired of bean soup. Bean soup. Bean soup. 'All they kept giving me was bean soup, and I'd had enough of it.' That's why he did it. All the years of being dished up bean soup without variation. He'd had enough.

He hid up in the scrub of the Yarra, just up, you know, where the bridge is, just over Studley Park Road. Just down in there. He had killed because he was sick and tired of bean soup.

'He what?'

Bean soup. Bean soup. 'All they kept giving me was bean soup, and I'd had enough of it.' That's why he did it. All the years of being dished up bean soup without variation. He'd had enough.

'So what happened to him?'

He was found not guilty by reason of insanity, to be detained at the Governor's pleasure. He could still be inside there. You've got to accept life, raw as it is. I had mortuary duties, drownings, shootings, and heart attacks. In my case, it was close family only. I was in bed when I had mine. I wasn't even working then.

The night before, I'd had a bit of pain. I sat up and it went away. Next night, the bloody pain came again and even that's got its funny side. I had a leg in plaster right up to the hip when I had the heart attack. I was putting plaster up with my son, John, when the ligament tore. Three-hour operation. So when I decided I was having a heart attack, I looked in the mirror to see if I was really having one. I chucked the crutch away and walked on the leg.

June comes over to sit with him and holds his hand and smiles at him.

June's driving. We get to Murray Road Preston and the lights are red, so June stops at the intersection. She stops.

And I said, 'What did you stop for?' She said, 'Red light.' I said, 'Fuck the fucking red light.'

When we got to the hospital, she was looking everywhere for a parking spot. I said, 'Park there' – there were empty spots just outside Casualty. She said, 'I can't park there. That's for emergency vehicles.' And I said, 'What do you think we are?'

I was okay in a couple of weeks. In ten days, I was up and running. I went to Canberra. There for two years. Got a contract to start. When they found out it was me, they didn't really want me. I had what you might call a reluctant retirement. Chief Superintendent rank.

About the Australian Federal Police. They see themselves as the FBI. (*Laughs ruefully.*) They're now called Agents, like in

America. Australian Federal Police only police Federal laws. They can't come to Victoria to investigate a murder.

Back to the albums again. These pictures are all in colour. In the '70s and '80s.

Here's Canada. With colleagues there in their office, see? Here's America. New York. It's a world brotherhood of police. Oh yes. Same sorts of problems all over the world. Lifestyle. Everything's the same. I'm glad I'm not in that job any more. I wanted to maintain the independence of the police force. I'd say to them, the bureaucrats, 'Are you instant experts? Leave it to us.' It's not the same any more, today. They can hardly walk today, coppers, with all the equipment on them.

He looks at me, square on, as if this is his final testimony, the last thing that he wants to say about all the things he's done, and all the things he's fought for. And what his efforts mean at the end of the day. And he says these things slowly, with appropriate weight, to summarise the faithful years of an old hard working copper.

I've tried to do my job honestly and to the best of my ability.

Have I listened to an old copper for an evening and a morning or a whole lifetime? All the anecdotes, all the rage, all the loneliness. At seventy-three, he's leaping into yet another dirty, empty building in search of crooks. His endless nemesis. The enemies he's dealt with over thirty-eight years. Dropping through plaster ceilings. Shinnying up and down drainpipes to catch illegal gamblers. Raiding massage parlours. The frustration of seeing Melbourne promote gaming, when he's just about killed himself – with others, of course – trying to break it up. He has one more word to add to his history with the force.

Bill Leaman, on the first major SP raid that the squad made, risked his life on the fifth-floor parapet at Chapel Lodge, St Kilda. It would've only taken one of the panic-stricken females inside to push to window open and he would've gone.

'What was it all for' he asks. But he's an idealist and a protector of our community.

Above: Gavin Warren with his wife

Gavin Warren

Joined Australian Federal Police 1988

Resigned as federal agent in 2000

'Chance favours only the prepared mind'

Gavin Warren – federal agent

I met Gavin Warren a few years ago at the Lost Dogs' Home in North Melbourne, where I was asked to give a reading from my children's book, *Joey: A Dog For All Seasons*. It wasn't so easy to give a live reading at this venue: although there was a good crowd of people who seemed appreciative of my efforts, the baying of lost dogs meant that finite comprehension came at a premium.

Afterwards I chatted with this friendly and open-hearted police officer about dogs being symbols for Australian writers. He said, 'This lost dog and cat shelter, mate, is the perfect place for loving words about pets', and we spoke of other aspects of life. Walking back to my home nearby, I wondered whether I'd ever see this gentle giant again?

Gavin Warren, at our first meeting, put the lie to any notion of 'police bastards' with his inscrutable sweetness and his vision of a friendlier, wider community. Since then, we have seen each other by chance, and after he granted me an interview to talk about his own police history, the next thing I knew, he was greeting me gigantically with large, twinkly eyes and leading me into his tiny terrace populated by once-lost-but-now-found cats and a single dog. Having brought no kids into an awful world by choice, Gavin and his wife have blossomed into protectors of lost animals such as the beautiful ones that were to keep us company throughout the entire interview.

Having patiently shown me how to put batteries into my cheap imported tape recorder, Gavin began chatting on about his working life with great ease and not a little drama, waving his great arms around the sitting-room like oars in a lake, with sound effects provided by the plop of armchair cushions and the meowing of rescued cats. I felt as if this slightly satiric situation was located in actual Heaven, where there were no crimes, no drugs and no loneliness of spirit.

Sipping the obligatory Nescafé, at one stage I asked Gavin whether or not he wore a weapon, and just then he seemed to want to scratch his left ankle through his sock. 'Well, this is where I hide it. A five-shot Smith & Wesson revolver. 'I wear it every moment I'm on duty.' It's so different seeing guns not in movies.

His is a large and expressive, strong face, with a near-perpetual beaming smile as authentic as his love and protection of neglected animals. He is highly moral and just so protective.

Citizens have lost their own plot. We seem to live in a time of hate against our own lot. People getting involved in fist fights in front of kids right in our own neighbourhoods, over trifling matters like insults or who has thieved someone else's personal parking space. Who cools us down? We put such pressure on our own children to be properly educated and beautifully read, but what about a beautiful neighbourhood, or are they mythical? I asked Gavin about these sorts of things – these conundrums – throughout the course of the conversation.

Personally, I felt a loneliness at his home, but this was due to the complete absence of children's laughter, a state of affairs I am no longer used to. Yet this silence only made me more aware of the difficulty of Mr and Mrs Warren's decision.

You don't want to bring innocent little kids into a world gone insane, do you? No, you don't!

Yes you do, if there is the possibility of a better world …

But my temporary feeling of loneliness was swiftly overcome by shared adult laughter and reflection. This man's a raconteur intellectual, I thought to myself. He's sweet and friendly without putting it on, his huge arms windmilling towards the kettle to tip boiling hot water onto more holy Nescafé. Like conversing with an octopus. It must be great to be so big. I have to say I felt in the thrall of really safe protection in his company.

The giant Warren gently plucked one of his three cats from the floor and stroked it playfully and lovingly.

This is Budweiser – he's the oldest. He was dumped at Melbourne Airport – picked up in the divvy van. The others are Marteka, and Sabrina, the one-eyed wonder.

I've just asked him: 'Can you start by describing the sort of police work you do and why?' when I look and there's a hare at my feet. He collects hares, too, and looks after them. Fancy that. A live hare here.

My rank's always been the same, although the name has changed over a number of years. I've been a constable, a detective constable, and now I'm a federal agent. I'm just a basic, everyday investigator. I spent nine years in the army and when I was driving, commanding armoured personnel carriers, we used to do a lot of reconnaissance, which is basically the same thing. But I've been in surveillance now for two and a half years. And it's something I've found I've got a real bent for. I've got the aptitude for it. I love the work. It suits my character.

Let me give you an example. One time, we went up to Echuca, following two characters from Sydney who were going across to Perth. They came down to Melbourne from Sydney to deal drugs, large quantities of them. In the back of their old Holden tray-back ute they had all sorts of things, even old tool boxes. But their load was 'grass' mainly – dope. It was fairly high-grade grass, which the Sydney AFP office and the National Crime Authority thought was maybe imported.

These two characters were staying in Euroa. Every morning we'd have to go up to Euroa at 6 am to start our surveillance and around three o'clock the afternoon shift would come up and relieve us. It went on like that for a week.

This one day I want to tell you about, we watched them

fuelling up the ute, checking the tyres, preparing for a big trip. When they started driving, they took all the back roads, and they were doing, oh, a maximum of ninety kilometres an hour. Now, as you can imagine, it's one of the hardest things in the world – to follow a car that's going under the speed limit, 'cause you stand out like a third nut on a greyhound.

Anyway, using all our surveillance skills, we got them up to Echuca, where they stopped in at the pub, by about an hour before dusk. I don't know whether they sold a few deals – we don't actually get that close when we're doing our work – but they left Echuca just on dusk, and about twenty, thirty minutes out of Echuca we lost them. We sort of let them get away a bit. You try to make it so that, just as they're going round the bottom corner, you're coming round the top corner, so you catch a glimpse every now and again. But we lost them. There were only two ways they could have gone: straight ahead on the highway, towards Mildura; or along one of a number of tracks towards the Murray.

One of our boys, Rabbit, saw the fading cloud of dust on one of the tracks and said, 'Right, that's where I think they've gone', and he sped up and took off down the highway to catch up with them. Which is what you usually do if you lose them: get someone up real quick – real, real quick – to try and find them.

But he didn't find them. By looking at the country maps we could see that there was a number of places they could have gone in there. So we waited a couple of hours until it got dark, and it was as dark as ... black as a dog's guts. It was a beautiful night – clear, no moon to speak of. And there was just a track, basically just a dirt road.

Although I've always been a bit of a city boy, I'm a bushy at heart. You know, I love the bush and I've spent a bit of time in it. So, being the only one with any real bush experience I said,

'Well, listen, boys, that's it. I'm going down there. I'll take my radio. I'll take my firearm.' And basically that's all I *could* take. I had a pair of dark blue overalls in the car. So off I trot ...

One of the cats tries to help with my note-taking...'Come here, you,' Warren says, gently plucking Sabrina up, never completely ignoring his charges ... At the same time never losing the thread.

Because we didn't know how far down they'd gone, I had to be careful from the start. I saw some rouseabouts on a farm, mustering up some cattle in the yard so I went and checked all the cars, everything in the outbuildings, the whole bit. They weren't there. And they weren't at the little house, at this little shack, probably a kilometre down the road. I was doing all this without any torch, because I didn't want to give myself away. Yeah, basically, I went one foot after the other, just creeping down this road.

I radioed the boys a couple of times, to keep them informed. 'Haven't found anything yet ... Haven't found anything yet ...' And then I could smell a campfire. That was it. I thought, 'Righto, I'm on the trail here.' I let the boys know, and told them, 'If you hear shooting, come in.' Surveillance is really a team job and you get good results with good teamwork.

I just followed my nose, basically, and kept to the track, which was a fairly well-worn bush track consisting of two ruts. I could make out car tyre marks, and it was dry, so when I walked I could feel the difference between the dirt and undergrowth – dry leaves and whatever. This made it easy to follow in the dark. When I got down to half a K from the Murray, the smell of smoke was stronger. And then I could then see light through the trees. It was just a little campfire, a very little campfire. I kept a nice big gum tree in between me and the fire at all times – old sniper training – and crept up on them. I got to within about fifteen, twenty metres. The watch I had used to beep on every hour, so I had let that go. But I reckon the last hundred yards would've taken me about an hour. Probably didn't take as long in reality, but it seemed that long.

I turned off my radio and squatted down behind the gum tree. That was a journey in itself, just squatting down and kneeling down. Move an inch –

'You don't want your knees to creak,' I quip. And the comment turns out to have some basis in reality. 'My oath,' Warren agrees. 'My old football-playing knees, they're buggered. Sound like a bag of Twisties.'

So I squatted down behind this tree, and I was listening to these guys talking – fifteen, twenty metres away. I was right on top of them. They were talking about having gone to Perth before, and 'yeah, I've done this trip many times'. I could tell the two different voices. One had a sort of high-pitched tone – for a man it seemed high-pitched; and the other guy had a real booming sort of deep, resonant voice. And I listened to the conversation probably for about half an hour, as they were getting on to the turps. One was drinking scotch, and one was drinking brandy, which I thought was odd. But they were drinking in a relaxed sort of way, not hosing it down. They were very relaxed. They weren't, as we say, toey. They weren't nervous or anything. They were just having a bit of a bonding session in the bush. Getting to know one another, I suppose.

I was probably about two minutes from pulling the pin and getting out of there when, for I don't know what reason, one of them picked up one of those Dolphin torches, and just swung it round, in a great big arc, and it was like sitting right in front of a lighthouse – you just know that beam's going to hit you. So I shuffled myself sideways as best I could, and hid behind this gum tree. Because it was a fairly still night, the smoke was hanging pretty heavy in the air. I could see the beam coming towards me like a solid object. And stop. Fifteen centimetres from my face. And you could just tell it was going to the other side of the tree. So I was in the shadow, the only place to be. And my heart, it was absolutely racing. I mean, these blokes weren't desperadoes or anything but we didn't know whether they had firearms, or shotguns or whatever. Not that I needed to worry – I had my firearm. And they're sitting around a fire, so they've got no night vision. I've got all the night vision. So I had the high ground.

'Was there any insect noise – crickets, or anything?'

Oh, there were crickets – all the normal bush noise. It was marvellous, actually, being in the bush at night. I could hear the scritter-scratter off in the distance. That's another thing you've got to be careful of, you know, you don't want to scare creatures towards them because that's one of the indicators.

'And when the bloke swept the Dolphin lamp around, did you think he was looking for anything?'

No, it was just one of those things. They hadn't used this torch all night.

'What happened next?'

I just froze for a fair while. Let them sort of settle back down. Listened to their conversation, made sure they were relaxed. They didn't even talk about shining the torch or anything, which was funny.

Then, not wanting to have any possible stuff-up whatsoever, I diddy-bopped out of there, backtracked. And once I got my hundred, hundred and fifty metres away I turned my radio back on and said 'I'm coming out' and called for a car to drive me out.

The car was about four kilometres in, off the main road. By the time we got back to the main road, it was four o'clock in the morning.

'You'd been there since dusk. You'd been there for nine hours or something.'

Basically a full day's work. I'd been waiting there, waiting, getting in, listening, waiting, coming out. And we have to work to budgets unfortunately – so all the boys said, 'Oh, we won't claim overtime for this,' cause they're just sitting, 'we'll claim what's called 'on-close call' allowance.' Which was fourteen bucks for the night, and bear in mind this is only two years ago. My hardest fourteen bucks ever. Then we started work the next day at eight o'clock. And those bush blokes drove out.

We let them drive out. As they drove down the track, we had the place surrounded – we had the intersection surrounded. As they took off, we kept following them, right on to Mildura, where they did more business. And then we followed them to Renmark where we had a rendezvous with the South Australian 'Dogs' (Dog Squad ... surveillance ... following people around like dogs) to hand them over.

It was actually an Australia-wide team effort. The New South Wales Dogs had brought this pair down to Victoria, we had them in Victoria, we took them to South Australia. I think they lost them at Wilpena Pound, from what I was told – they lost them for a week or so. So these blokes really did go bush. Eventually they made it to Perth, and they did their business there and were later arrested back in Sydney some two or three months later. I think it ended up a National Crime Authority job, which means there were state cops involved, and Federal Police.

All of the Dogs did exactly the same as we had done – same objective: just to find them, follow them, and document.

I mean, all the Dogs do is observe and make notes, take photographs and videos, whatever they can do. Professional witnesses, that's what we are. But there are blokes in the Dogs who just don't have it. We have trouble getting people to actually come into the Dogs.

'It's a calling, isn't it?'

It is. It impinges on your private life. You're on permanent shift work...it's a pain in the arse.

'And what's it worth salary-wise?' I can feel a moist nose in my thigh. A found dog.

Well, last year I got about fifty-four for the year, but that was with all my penalties and a bit of overtime. The Federal Police want to make surveillance a lower paid job than investigations. Admittedly, to be good in investigations you've got to have skills, you've got to have natural aptitude. Talent, that's a given; you've got to be a smart cookie. But with surveillance, you've got to be cunning. You've got to be stealthy. Yeah, you've just got to have the aptitude for it.

'Who's the best teacher you've ever had – someone who was your inspiration, a guru?'

The guru of surveillance is a man known as 'Badger', who now works for the Western Australian Corruption Commission. He was in Federal Police. He's only just got out and joined this 'boutique agency', as a general manager in Victoria called it.

I think Badger's greatest gift is his calmness. He's just so calm about it all. I mean, it's easy to get excited, especially when you're driving around like a mad thing. Yes, it's his calm. Nothing fazes him too much. And in Melbourne he was like the Talking Melway. Unbelievable knowledge of Melbourne. We'd be driving through an area, which I knew we hadn't been in in a year or eighteen months, and he'd be calling – on the radio, you make calls, saying things like 'coming up to Market Street', 'on Epsom Road, travelling west', 'coming up to Smithfield Road' and so on. Well, Badger would call the little side streets as well, from two hundred metres away down the road. Absolutely phenomenal. He's a brilliant guy. He's also an arachnophobe, unfortunately. He wouldn't get out of the car in the bush, even if the car was on fire.

'How was he towards you?'

You actually had to earn your lumps, earn your stripes with him. I did a couple of silly things in my first year, which is when you tend to earn more ire than respect. Your superiors quickly get a bit pissed off with you if you make silly calls, if you don't know where you are, and stuff like that. On one of my very first jobs, we had to go to Braeside Avenue, Ringwood. I went to Braeside Drive, Braeside. That's probably only twenty-five kilometres out of my way!

He pauses for the cat again. 'Are you all right, Sabrina? Are you okay?'

So they nicknamed me 'Braeside' and were calling me this for a while. You see, you have to earn their respect.

On that Braeside job, I had really been sent to Coventry. It was the first day I'd been given a car, and I was sort of solo. It was a controlled delivery of amphetamines. Took the box to the boy, and he took it to a hotel, the Waltzing Matilda Hotel, in Springvale. And they said, 'All right, Tex [Tex is my usual nickname]. Righto, Texy, get around the back of the pub. Stay behind the fence, stay out of sight.' So I did. Then I took my camera out. I was just having a bit of a play with it through a hole in the back fence of the Waltzing Matilda Hotel, just lining it up. It was a thirty-five mill Nikon; you know, with the motor drive – getting the light settings right, playing with the focus and everything, and, sure enough, there's a bloke walking up the steps with a box. So I took a few photographs of him: click, click, click. The box had a big orange sticker on it. I think it was Federal Express we used that day as a courier. So, yes, big orange FedEx sticker on it. Couldn't miss it.

What I didn't know was that the boys had lost him in the car park. And the only photographs we ever got were the man with the hands on the drugs. Eighteen months later I was in court proving those photographs. That was a big sealer. I was pretty proud of those photos, the way they came out.

'And how are the accused shown these photographs?'

Well, in the record of interview, when the chap's been arrested, the detectives are talking to him, and they say something like 'Righto, well we've got these photographs of you. There you go. Walking up the stairs with your hands on the drugs. Hands on the box containing the drugs.'

'What do they say back to that? What can they possibly say? 'It's not my good side'?' Gavin Warren laughs.

Exactly. I mean, that's the beauty of photography. 'Oh, I need a new haircut, don't I?' And that's another thing. When you see them in court – short back and sides, nice blue suit – being compared with the photograph of the guy in the flannelette shirt, you know, the Death Metal t-shirt, ripped up jeans, long hair, and, 'Nuh! It's not the same person, can't be the same person.'

The Waltzing Matilda photos got me a little bit of kudos. Made up for Braeside. But, actually, the Echuca bush trip – that got me the most kudos, with 'Badger' especially. He even took me out later that morning, by which time I was totally shagged.

He took all of us out for breakfast. It is very unlike 'Badger' to shout. Wouldn't shout if a shark bit him.

Praise from him meant a great deal. He said to me, that night, 'This is going to go down in Dog history.' So it has become part of surveillance folklore. Oh, you know, I was over the moon, absolutely over the moon. Later he was a guest instructor at one of the basic surveillance courses, and in one of the lessons he gave, he emphasised the point of doing all you can do, being the best Dog that you can be, and using every skill that you've got, and then he used the bush trip as an example. Just getting in there and doing it.

It seems to me as an outsider that, when you're putting your life at risk, like in that campfire scenario, you're not feeling anything especially against the criminals. It's more a question of discovery.

Yes, that's what it is. There's no animosity between us and the crooks. You'll hear state cops speaking of crims with a real animosity – it's an us-against-them attitude. But with the Dogs, it's different. You know, we're happy for the suspects to go around doing what they do, as long as they stand in the light and give us good, nice profiles, nice smiles. I've got some great photographs.

If those two blokes at Echuca had thought they heard an insect sound and had started to move towards you, armed or whatever, what would have been the next step be in the procedure?

The hypotheticals could go either way. You can either hitch up real quick, or, rather than run, you can hop and try not to make a sound (you don't go crash, crash, crash, crash, I'm running through the bush). If you sort of take a step ... step ... step ... like that [*he mimes a roo in his sitting-room – most impressive*], you can sound like a kangaroo hopping. That's an old trick. An old army trick – you make more of a one-step, and you don't go real fast. And then I'd have been out of there –

'What other sort of police work have you done?'

Early in my career, I spent two years in uniform at Melbourne Airport. I was then hand-picked by the Commander of Fraud and General Crime to go the Fraud and General Crime Unit. The first three months I spent as a bodyguard for a Family Court judge. (Don't know why. I'm only six foot four.) We still have a duty to protect the Family Court because it's a federal court. It's our jurisdiction. And it's very volatile. You try not to think of what can happen, and respond to what does. But you've got to be awake. I mean, being a policeman, you've got to be very awake, and alert, and ... have an intuition.

'What were your daily duties?'

Court security. Make sure the judge gets in and out. I actually went on a lot of circuits. I did Geelong a couple of times. Albury–Wodonga a couple of times. Wagga. You know, wherever the judges would travel, I'd go travel them. And it was good. Anyway, so I'd set up the court, then, after work, the New South Wales Law Society would take the judge out and I'd do an advance reconnaissance on the restaurant, or wherever they were going. I'd work out two exits, introduce myself to the man-ager – you know, 'we want this table' ... you've just got to arrange all these contingencies.

In that sort of work, you've got to be able to relate to people. Got to be able to talk to anyone, no matter what their station in life. You know, it could be someone asking you directions, or it could be the United States Ambassador.

Well that's not such a simple skill. That's something that comes from a sort of a special charm. Charm's unteachable, isn't it?

It certainly is. Just as experience is unteachable. It's just contact with people. Probably the best two years' training, or grounding, as a police officer I got was at Melbourne Airport, in uniform. We had rotating shifts, so you'd do day shift, afternoon shift, night shift. One day per shift, you'd do in the control room, as a radio operator, a computer operator. Then you'd do everything, from the security of the airport in general, to jumping into the divvy van and performing traffic duties. Everything a community policeman does, we would do there, but just within the precinct of the airport.

And you can't get away from people. You can't ignore people if you're six foot four and wearing a big blue shirt and a big white hat with a black-and-white band around it. People come up to you and ask you the most stupid questions. You just smile and say, 'Yes sir, No sir, Three bags full sir – The drinking fountain is over there, where that little tap thing is.' You can't lose your patience. You know, somebody asks you for the time ... You think 'What do I look like? Friggin' Big Ben?' But you don't say it.

You've just got to keep calm, like 'Badger'. His motto – and we still say it, almost daily – was 'Results, not excuses'. And that's all he'd say. He'd say that over the radio. If you started, 'Well, aw, I was doing this and something happened ...' you'd just hear his same old voice: 'Results ... not excuses ...' Or, just 'Results'.

I live by mottoes. I mean, I love that one. I've got a number of them. But my personal motto is actually a quote from Louis Pasteur. It's 'Where observation is concerned, chance favours only the prepared mind.' I'm going up to Canberra to be trained in advanced surveillance technique, and I'm going to try to have that adopted as the official surveillance motto. We don't have a logo, we don't have a motto, we don't have anything. We're just ... the Dogs. But I think Louis Pasteur knocked the nail right on the head.

I live by mottoes. I've got a number of them. But my personal motto is a quote from Louis Pasteur. It's 'Where observation is concerned, chance favours only the prepared mind.' I think Pasteur knocked the nail right on the head.

Brian Ritchie, the last cop to arrest Ronald Ryan in Melbourne, is quoted as having said, when he was at Footscray, that they were losing the war on drugs. (I think he was a superintendent there at that stage.) Do you think that that's still the case, or are there signs where it's not that way any more?

I think we're still losing the war on drugs. I can tell you from my perspective, which is city-wide really, that the drugs have got a lot cheaper. They've got much cheaper and much purer. And, you know, there are more deaths. It's just about neck-a-neck with the road toll, isn't it?

And there's a global drug-producing community. Just to give you a thumbnail sketch of the global implications of drug cultivation, an opium poppy crop comes to fruition in ninety days. That's a fairly short production cycle. It's just the flowers – the bulbs and the flowers. Historically, the crops have always been grown in Thailand, Burma, Laos – you know, the Golden Triangle. That and the Middle East. The Colombians have always been the cocaine producers, the coca plants up in the Andes. That's the climate for it. They've discovered that they can get better crop rotation with an opium crop, and they're actually producing their own opium. Heroin is derived from that. The opium and heroin trade is now coming out of Colombia and out of South America, and that's going straight up to North America, Mexico, the United States and Canada. Therefore, the Asian heroin trade to North America, the United States, has actually dried up a bit. And they're dumping it on their nearest neighbour, which is us. And that's actual f-a-c-t – fact. There's been a glut, and it's been happening for a few years.

Real dogs are scampering outside, reminding us of humbler, more innocent realities. Gavin Warren says to his own dog, 'Come here. You just be quiet, okay? [The dog hurumphs.] You speak when you're spoken to. [The dog whines.] Do you want to go out for a wee?' The dog replies, apparently in the affirmative. I know how he feels, as I suddenly realise how long I have been absorbed in conversation with this genial man, and how much instant coffee we have consumed. 'It was better in some ways,' I reflect, 'when the old fashioned traffickers thinned the drugs, because they kept the junkies alive.'

Kept *some* of them alive, exactly right.

'Is that why some of the kids are keeling over now?'

It is. Because sometimes when they do cut it, you know, they cut it with glucose, Ratsack, who knows ... They don't do it properly. There's no quality assurance, there's no quality control in the drug trade. So instead of when they did have to mix it down to ten per cent (when I joined, drug purities were about ten per cent, ten to twelve, something like that), now, you can arrest someone with a sample that is sixty to seventy per cent pure. But some of them don't mix it properly. A lot of the young dealers don't know how to get the whisk, and whisk it out, do all that stuff.

'Over your twelve years, since you've started with the police, has anything particularly saddened you – shaken you up or touched you? What's got to you?'

Yes, absolutely. I was down in Springvale, sitting watching a target (or customer, or whatever you want to call it) – the subject of our surveillance, who was doing some shopping at the

Springvale shops. And I was sitting in the car park, looking after his car, making sure that car didn't just get up and disappear. I was just in a plain old, very plain Jane sedan, and I had the seat flipped back, like I was asleep. I was watching a guy go round the back of the carpark, the back wall of the car park at the Springvale shops, picking up all the used needles. And I thought, 'Ah, this guy's doing a public service, cleaning up.' And he was picking them up for twenty minutes, half an hour, till he had a fistful of needles, like he couldn't close his hand around them – all these old, discarded syringes. I thought, that is just sensational. He was a scruffy looking character.

He then went into a little alcove area, pulled out of his pocket a bottle of Mount Franklin spring mineral water and started sucking water into each of these syringes ... mixed it up in a little polystyrene cup ... shot it straight into his arm.

He was after the residue. He was like the nineties version of one of the old hoboes who used to pick up all the old cigarette butts and dog ends. He shot the stuff up into his arm, and I don't know what he got out of it ... but I just thought that was the most pitiful thing I'd ever seen. I felt a real sense of pity, and a sense of waste. It was a mixed emotion. It was so depressing to see that.

That would have been about eighteen months ago. And, it's always with me, that memory. I'll never forget that. Who knows what he would have caught. No respect for his health.

I consider animals of the world to be the only true innocents left. I put all my energies into animal charities. Not that I don't like people; I do... But people have a choice. You have a choice whether you stick a needle in your arm, or rob someone, or pull a knife or a gun. Animals can't make those choices, so it takes people like me to look after them.

'Do you think the world has become more selfish? That people are looking after themselves more than they are looking after the community? It's a lonely world for some.'

It is. I mean, my wife and I, we love our animals. We don't have any children – by choice. I'm cynical and I say, 'Oh, I wouldn't want to bring kids into this world', but I've got friends who are having children, and I'm happy for them. I'm just not a children sort of person.

Look, we subscribe to animal charities, the WSPCA, the RSPCA, the Lost Dogs' Home. I consider animals of the world to be the only true innocents left. I put all my energies into animal charities. Not that I don't like people; I do like people – I'm a people person. But people have a choice. You have a choice whether you stick a needle in your arm, or rob someone, or pull a knife or a gun. You know, there are conscious choices that we make. Animals can't make those choices, so it takes people like me to look after them. You don't have a choice as a dog. You have no choice in what you do.

Gavin Warren gently shows me how to stop the tape, and our time together is over.

Anne Wregg
Joined Victoria Police 1969
Awarded Queen's Gallantry Medal 1976
Completed detective training course 1977
Resigned as senior constable 1982

Just like Uncle Tony

Anne Wregg – former senior constable

It's pleasant enough, for a change, to conduct a police interview at Ricketts Point, the outdoor tea-room being just the shot after what feels like millennia in airless and antiseptic back rooms of various police headquarters – places where no sea air or laughter comes. It's a beautiful day for conversation and reflection.

Anne Wregg and I shake hands. She looks fit and unmistakably Italian, with her dark skin and deep brown eyes. Very still and certain with gestures, emphatically alive to the fact of life and all of its promises. It's also good to get away from Anglo coppers for a change and tune in to the music of her voice. My own nasal vocal range has always saddened me, but you have to press on.

'I'm from San Marco, Italy. You've heard of it?' she says to me as she sips a frothy white coffee.

Came over on the boat in '56. Dad was out here beforehand, so other members of the family were here first. Then my mother and the rest of us came over. Over a month, the boat took. I was nine when you work it out.

She fiddles with a blue Biro on notepaper. Doodling and so on.

When I saw the shores of Australia, all I saw was bush! I'm going back to '57 and '58. We persisted. We lived in Ardmona, where my Dad got work. My Dad was a share-farmer, to begin with, at the Ardmona company. Tomatoes, fruit, dairy cows. Dad worked pretty hard, all right.

I sip some sparkling mineral water and take in our setting. Comfortable middle-class Anglo–Saxon Australians sit nibbling chicken sandwiches and red lettuce, no one bothered by money or life. Poverty seems a joke. But not then.

So too did my brother work hard. They put in some pretty tough hours. My father ruled with an iron fist. Up at half past six. He knocked on all of our doors and said 'Zavati!' That means 'Get up!' So we were up and ready to pick tomatoes.

It was Mum who brought the espresso machine over from the Old Country, and it was her coffee that used to wake us.

His breakfast? Home-made Italian biscuits baked by my Mum and an earlier form of home-made caffe latté: milk and coffee mixed together. For us, too – percolated coffee is my first memory. It was Mum who brought the espresso machine over from the Old Country, and it was her coffee that used to wake us.

With the tomatoes, you had to do so many boxes. I can recall there was a fine green dust came off them. You'd feel itchy by the end of the day. If we found rotten tomatoes, we threw them away. Mixed wine and vinegar to ward off the flies, which are something shocking at Ardmona. You don't put on much, just a thin film. Mum was allergic to mozzies. She'd come up in all these welts, like water blisters. She was a country girl, but she hated the countryside here. 'Too straggly,' she said. She hated the way people's heels cracked through their stockings, how their hands cracked from the harshness of the sun.

She says it was family teamwork got them going, despite the hardship of the farm.

Mum cooked, made the salami home-style ... pickles, anything. I can do all that, too, thanks to her. All of my brothers can cook well, too. When we sat at the dinner table we all talked, as little children – we had our say. We drank wine and liqueur moderately at a very young age. Dad'd mix home-made red wine mixed with lemonade.

It all sounds perfectly democratic and splendidly exuberant.

We picked for Rosella's – the sauce company, you know. We had to make sure we stacked the big boxes properly. Twenty-five kilos in weight they were. Dad kept on talking to the boys when we picked the tomatoes but he never sang.

Leave that to the romantic films about workers of the world ...

We only did that sort of work for eight or nine months. Then we came to Melbourne and a favourite uncle lent my father 3250 pounds for a house. Do I ever remember the cost of the way he paid Uncle Tony back for lending the money for our first house!

It all had to be in one repayment, you know, not paid back piece-meal, a fraction at a time.

She has temporarily lost her breath.

> *I loved running! I had to beat everyone else. I can remember going through the tape and they said 'Stop, you've already won. You've already been through it.' But I kept on going, kept on winning.*

We attended Saint Monica's Catholic School in Footscray – 1957. On our first day there we actually saw the parish priest! We still see each other, as a matter of fact. Father John Herriot is his name. He was, and is still, a fantastic man. He spoke a little Italian, so he was very welcome in those days.

Dad thought sport was for people who never work, so no sport for him, and he didn't want us to do sport, either. But I won the fifty-yard sprint in those days. Down at Myers Flat, it was, in Footscray. I loved running! I had to beat everyone else. I can remember going through the tape and they said 'Stop, you've already won. You've already been through it.' But I kept on going, kept on winning.

Dad was a cheese-maker by trade but he never received the chance to do what he was good at. A quarry was where he worked, earning about three pound ten shillings a week. He caught the bus to work. He used to say to us kids 'I never want you children to do what I've done to make a living.'

Cosy, comfortable middle-class patrons sip delicate chowder in harmony. The cash register sips their pay. I want to move in. Everything's so easy here and delicious.

One big treat when I was a child growing up was we'd pour hot milk over Teddy Bear biscuits so they'd enlarge. No butter on the bread, just a thin wafer of home-made Italian jam.

We ate Weet-Bix and skim milk in stoney silence.

We'd come home at lunch-time and have a French loaf of bread, you know. We'd scoop half of the lovely soft white bread out, then Mum'd drop an omelette in it. Parmesan cheese over fresh country eggs. Then Mum'd chop up a fresh sprig of parsley and add the green shoots of fresh garlic. It had to have Mum's Mozzarella in it!

We had Kraft.

Mum's favourite recipe for illness was chamomile flowers suffused in boiling hot water. She suffered bad migraines and those flowers really worked!

I enjoy chamomile too. But we had Bushell's.

There was a Mrs Binns at the local lolly shop who gave you big bags of broken biscuits, not just a bit full but overflowing with broken biscuits. You know, topped up. We never missed out on food! Mum'd create a banquet right in front of us: out of nothing! An old-fashioned Italian family.

Our first friends in Footscray were the La Manna family – Calabrians. A different dialect. All kids understood all dialects!

She laughs passionately. Yes, you're quite right about that.

We used to frequent others' places all the time. We played 'chasey'. Cricket was played on the street. I can never recall any of my brothers fighting. My father laid down the law and said 'You never *ever* fight!'

Tight-lipped. Tough. That's it. He ruled.

But a friend of one of my brothers insulted me and made a pass at me. So I pulled him off his bike and gave him a whack he wouldn't easily forget. In those early years I was skinny and wiry.

Our local fish-and-chip shop used to have a bar-type counter with stools and we'd watch 'The Cisco Kid' on the old black and white overhead TV. Westerns, you know.

I didn't know what I wanted to do with myself when I was fifteen. Dad had always said 'Go to school and do well!' As to boys, I never went out with any. You just didn't then in a strict Italian family. We'd go off to Mass. With Italians the trend gets passed on. There's no mystery to religion. Nothing's explained and you just believe.

She leans on her wrist. Munches some lettuce. Brilliant white teeth snap.

When I left school in '63 I worked in a bank. I joined the Force in 1969, and that same year my mum was killed in a car crash.

She goes momentarily blank and I cannot think of a single word to say. People sip mineral water and chat. It suddenly seems moronic here because of the depth of Anne Wregg's feeling.

I guess I must've had a strong feeling for having my hands in and helping the community from the start. I just wanted to do something that makes a difference. I had been going to join Alitalia Airlines. (*Laughs.*) But my father gave me the biggest lecture. 'If you do that – work as a hostess – you're going to be sworn at all the time!'

'And cursed,' she adds, paraphrasing.

He thought policing wasn't for women, either. I had to bide my time before telling him. I figured that if I took a career I wouldn't be stuck to someone. You know, get cronied off to some old codger in marriage! I remember I told my mother first that I had decided to join the Force – that was political. She said 'I can't believe how your father's going to react.'

My first meeting with a police officer? Let me think about that for a while.

She smiles and the people at the other tables seem to smile.

Well, Mum sent us on a message to the shops and we bought a Tatts ticket – you know, a lottery ticket. When we came home we had to say we didn't have any change. We said we'd spent it. Got a clip over the ears for that.

A few days later a great big policeman came to our door. Immediately Mum thought someone in the family had done something wrong! The policeman said: 'Are you the Cursio family?' (Cursio is our family name. Wregg is my married name; my husband was in the Force.) He'd come to our place because we'd won third prize in the Tattersall's lottery! Mum gave me a belt like you would not believe, right in front of that copper in the family doorway.

It was about two hundred pounds, we won. Mum still didn't believe it as she completed the form you have to sign and hand in.

'What made you choose policing?'

Look, I was just busting to be a policewoman! Uncle Tony, in Modena in Italy, he was a policeman. I used to sing out to the family 'I want to be just like Uncle Tony!' And they'd say, the old family 'But Uncle Tony is a man! You are a woman!' Mum was more or less on my side. As to Dad's acceptance of me, a young woman joining the Force? Dad really surprised me when he accepted my decision. Yes, he relented, he was quick to do that – relent and see how much I loved it, becoming something important. To do good.

He did lecture me on what to expect, though. He used to read the news in *Il Globo*, the Italian newspaper, from front cover to back.

When he first came to Australia people would say 'Oh, you're Italian!' As though to say 'So, you're with the Mafia, I believe?' And Dad would say 'Oh, well, the Mafia? Do we have it in our family?' To which we would all say nothing, as we weren't con- nected with them. Dad only knew about the Mafia what he read in the papers – about those men slain in the Grape Murders in the 60s at the Victoria Market.

I remember the grisly Sun News Pictorial *photographs. It was a famous case in which the Melbourne Mafia executed some sellers of grapes made for wine and sold at the market.*

I was twenty when I joined the police. At that time you were supposed to be twenty-one. I was the youngest woman in my intake. My Dad knew I was a naïve young lady. I wanted to know how many young women were joining. He did too. The other aspect of it was that I was Italian. And of course I wanted my Dad to be proud of me. Of course I did!

She trails off and looks at tea sippers doing nothing. God it must be nice to be rich and never work again in your life. Anne Wregg's eyes are bright with the past and the hope of the future.

To prove myself, I joined in March of '69. The accident was not even a year later.

My Mum and Dad decided they'd have my sister visit us from overseas. I recall the time so clearly. I was stationed at Russell Street – Policewomen's Division. Mum had to have everything just right, everything Italian, everything just like at home! Get all the right coffee roasted for the occasion (there was a special place for this in Moreland Road).

Mum died instantly. Dad was in Royal Melbourne for over ten months ... I was more determined than ever after the accident to make a difference.

We're all getting ready for the big banquet, a reunion celebration, it's going to be the biggest event in our lives, just about. It had to have been early in the morning. Dad was driving. A truck was going in the same direction and it tried to make a right-hand-turn from the left-hand lane and Dad swerved to miss it. Dad accelerated and lost control of the family car and hit a power pole.

His face, you should've seen his face! He had a sports steering wheel in that car and it shattered straight into his face in a hundred fragments. Mum died instantly. Dad was in Royal Melbourne for over ten months. In that time he probably experienced thirty-five operations. The first visit he got bolts through the jaw. His head was the size of a double pillow.

And the silvery-white hair on him became just a pale crewcut after that. (*She shows me an old-fashioned family portrait with all the children and the beautiful young optimistic father from the Old Country.*) That silvery-white stubble crewcut of his was the only thing about him I could recognise when we visited our father. And this was right on the eve of our big reunion. Our big party. I was more determined than ever after the accident to make a difference.

Who was my superior at the time? Grace Brebner; she was the Officer-in-Charge. She put the paperwork through for compassionate leave. This was not so much women's solidarity but the solidarity of the whole Force in general. I'd only been there twelve months. It felt like a second family. Grace really looked after me!

I was away a month or a month and a half. There was no Valium available in those days. You had a cup of tea and a lie down. That was seen as the cure for a nervous breakdown – not that I was having one. The old question applied then, and still does: when are you fit to go back to work? Grace Brebner called me in to the office. She said 'The door's always open.'

Day shift I did as a junior constable. Did prisoner escort. You went to the various country stations. You'd see to female prisoners being escorted from Ballarat to the courts in Melbourne. Take them to Magistrate's Court or the Children's Court – all the courts. In a police car or van – they called those vans 'brawlers'. There'd be Protection Applications, Protection Orders, parents out looking for their kids. One policewoman would be stationed at Ballarat or Bendigo. Hundreds of square miles were covered.

I remember one really magnificent tough girl at that time. I was on afternoon shift at Russell Street, where the prisoners go into the cells, and I had to search this female. About three in the afternoon it was. There was a senior constable and a constable there, and one of them said to me 'You can do this search.'

She was in bra and underwear, just standing there looking at me, with a 'What are you going to do now?' kind of expression on her face. To my complete horror, there were the most unusual tattoos across her chest. Roses and ... the tattoos were so dark, I thought 'Why have you had these done to your skin? Such a beautiful girl!'

As I went down the body I came across two tattoos, one on each of her upper thighs. One said 'Pay As You Enter'. The other said 'No Meat On Friday'. She was a pretty switched-on, streetwise young lady of about twenty or so. I thought 'Looking like that you'd spoil your afternoon at the beach.'

In about July of 1970 I was in the Drug Squad. I went up into the CIB for just a short time. That developed into full-time duties with the CIB. And I was in various squads after that: the Breaking Squad, Homicide. My superior was Rex Hornbuckle. I was the only girl attached to the CIB at the time.

Then the extortion case came up. It was Sir Reginald Ansett who was the target – his Melbourne office received threatening letters. Blackmail, in other words. Sir Reginald referred this matter to Russell Street Headquarters.

The extortionist demanded that certain instructions be followed. Some of the details included the fact that the money had to be handed over to a female employee of Sir Reginald's; otherwise the extortionist would blow up an Ansett plane. There'd be other bombs placed either in an airport or a plane somewhere. Some of the demands went through as Surface Mail. Otherwise it was in the form of a code he wrote and printed in the newspaper for us to follow.

Mr Reg Jackson was Commissioner of Police at the time. And Mick Patterson was in charge of Crime. I was asked to come to a briefing. There were some details and instructions that I had to know. Commissioner Jackson gave the briefing. On the second floor of Russell Street, this was.

The extortionist was taken seriously. My instructions were that I had to be dressed in such a way that he would recognise me. A red beret was a key part of the dress. And he wanted me to be dressed totally in black.

He was sweaty and nervous. I was instructed to keep him in conversation. He was a dark man. Olivey complexion, moustache; about thirty-five. I had the bag.

I was to meet him in Sydney in the airport departure lounge coffee shop. I had flown up with plain-clothes officers. I had on a black crew-neck jumper and a pair of black slacks – with the red beret, of course. And I had to say certain things that he'd written. He'd say 'Are you so-and-so?' To which I'd say 'Yes.' I had to say 'Are you him?' and he said 'Yes.'

He was sweaty and nervous. I was instructed to keep him in conversation. He was a dark man. Olivey complexion, moustache; about thirty-five. I had the bag. It was supposed to have $600,000 in it, but there were just a few notes on the top.

We had a coffee, for which he paid. (*Laughs.*) I suppose he was a gentleman in that sense. He offered me a cigarette. He had on shades and was very nervous. I didn't smoke or drink, but I had to smoke with him and just keep on chatting away. And then he wanted me to go with him and he said 'We've got enough money to see us out!' I refused.

'Why don't you come with me?' he beseeched. ' I've booked a ticket to Brisbane.' Then he said 'When are you going to hand over that bag with all the money in it?'

I said 'I'll hand you the money at the point of entrance. He agreed to that.

'Did it occur to you that he might have been armed and could simply shoot you there?'

It occurred to me, but I had to do my job.

'Were there Sydney plain-clothes officers, as well as your Melbourne colleagues, at the airport coffee shop?'

Yes, there were. Briskly he was duped. Then I handed the bag to him at the door and he was escorted from the plane. It all took about ten or fifteen minutes, but it seemed more like about two hours at least! I was a bit nervy, I suppose. The car was on the tarmac.

When I came home again late that same night my parents didn't know I had been involved (my Mum was still alive at the time). But the media got wind of it and had gone to my parents' home. The offender was charged with sending threatening letters. He got deported to South Africa. That was thirty years ago. After that experience every time I go to Sydney airport I think of him.

For Dad, it was something that an Italian coming out from another country had achieved.

Anne Wregg is retired from police work now and, with her husband, runs a florist's. Her working life is rather hectic and full.

I received the Queen's Gallantry Medal for my part in that. The Queen had actually been in Canberra six months before, so we didn't meet. It was a shame, in a way, that I couldn't receive my medal from the Queen personally. But never mind. It was by special invitation, the ceremony. Only two members of my family were present at Government House: my father and younger brother. The best moment of my life was my father seeing that in 1976. (He's still alive, my dad, actually. He's ninety.) For Dad, it was really something that an Italian coming out from another country had achieved. And he said, with his tears, something greater than words. The day I accepted the medal was the greatest day of my life.

Frank Holland, whom I am to interview next, believed in this modest and bright policewoman, and was responsible for sending her to Scotland Yard early in her career. A quiet and heroic soul, she has worked in many facets of policing, always applying her philosophy of duty combined with family honour. Now, her son wants to be a policeman, so the baton looks like being passed on, in true Italian family tradition.

After our conversation, we stand and shake hands in a friendly way. As we stroll away I smile at all the oblivious coffee and sandwich people and wonder if they fully that they understand what the police do for them.

Frank Holland

Joined Victoria Police 1935

Retired as commander 1975

The old days and now

Frank Holland

When he retired in 1975, Frank Holland had contributed forty years to the Victoria Police. Ninety-one recruits, there were, in his old squad. He did foot duty and wireless patrol, and once he organised a special group of police to handle abortion inquiries, when abortion was illegal. Indeed, every aspect of police work has fallen to Mr Holland. He's a kind of mentor or godfather to the Victoria Police.

An investigator of 128 murders and a natural scholar, he assisted in the apprehension of fugitive Pentridge Prison felon Ronald Ryan, who was hanged in 1967. He has received many valour awards over his long years of active service, including the Queen's Police Medal and a Chief Commissioners' Certificate for efficiency, loyalty and devotion to duty. Not surprisingly, I entered his flat in Glenhuntly Road, Elsternwick, somewhat awed by his position in police history. But he was courteous and friendly, and spontaneously reminisced over his education and other matters.

The flat is full to the brim with interesting volumes and histories relating to policing, among them the essential but obscure publication *How to Recognise and Handle Abnormal People: a manual for the Police Officer*, by Robert A. Mathews, MD, and Loyd W. Rowland, PhD, published some time ago by the National Association For Mental Health Inc. in New York.

Frank Holland relaxes, holding a stack of old manila folders and photocopies of clippings and so on. He is tall and careworn and craggy – and very deliberate about facts, as you would expect. He folds his big old hands together and squints at me, sitting upright in suit and tie at eighty-six years old, his shoes slightly rocking. A kettle relaxes also on its ancient jet in sympathy. The tiny flat is not ornate.

The dossiers are on a fold-up card table, all spread out for our scrutiny. His voice is a trifle croaky but still clear. There's no beating about the bush and his every word is explicit.

Well, I was born in 1915, at Flemington in Melbourne. My school was the local Christian Brothers in North Melbourne. It's still there. As a matter of fact I left school at fifteen. As boys at that school we exactly followed instructions. They'd indicate leaders in our class. They were always looking out for natural leaders – that was expected. They kept at us; and you were grateful.

He swings those long feet on those long legs. He quarter-smiles and peers into his coffee cup, as though searching for information. The long strong old body accompanying the spare and spartan words.

My father was an MP: the Labor Member for Flemington. When he retired, he was so sick he just died. In our family there were two boys and five girls, altogether. Mum looked after the lot.

He gazes away but overhead there's only a ceiling and memory. Nothing wrong with either.

In a real sense, home was pretty disciplinarian. We lived in the house. Life was sport and St Brendan's. I played footy. My brother was a great footballer.

Folds his arms and smooths out a sleeve-button or two on the end of it. His home has a great stillness. But he seems very active, to say the least – almost too big for the flat.

Mum made sure we all read. She was a schoolteacher – had taught the lot until she married Dad.

Breathes and relaxes to summon things back to life. His friendly face is pink and freckled.

Our old family, we helped people to obtain work during the Depression. Mum and Dad originated a meal thing for the poor people of the Flemington–Kensington area, at Kensington Town Hall. Poverty didn't mean too much to you then, unless it was you personally who was suffering from it. You weren't allowed to make comments about any of it, life, in those days. You watched it. From a distance.

A few trips, you had, excursion-wise. There was a launch, a boat went up the Maribyrnong River. In those days – the Depression – a lot of homes in that area were just tents, old tents and boxes people lived in. A shanty town, it was. It was called Dudley Flats. It was pretty down.

And he looks down now at his floor in harmony. As if to see those people again somehow.

Fruit boxes, people used for doors – that sort of thing. They improvised this was the case for a lot of poor people living in Melbourne until about 1940.

M'grandfather was a copper in Victoria. He died in the early 90s; the *eighteen* nineties, that is. M'uncle joined. In Parkville. He was Thomas Christopher Holland. He became a Detective – Detective-Sergeant. Had cancer. Died. But before he died he was in charge of the old Motor Registration Branch. He had his right hand removed. His right hand was pretty bad but he still managed to stick a Biro into it to write with. I can't remember my grandfather too well, just that one particular memory.

He leans across to examine me. Sits upright again with that stiff old back of his, ramrod straight, and this gently old-world voice of his, whiling away the afternoon. He is living police history, no doubt of it. A very rare old gentleman.

In 1935 I joined the police force. Oh, well! I wanted to join. (*This is shouted.*) Dad said 'Get examined!' So I did. And that was it! I was in perfect nick. I'd just turned twenty. Right on the mark. I was five foot ten and fighting fit. Fit as a mallee bull!

Cops in the old times were allowed to smoke, but not on duty... Bloody Hell, where is it? I wanted to show you a book. Wanted to show it to you, this book of mine. Now where on earth is it?

I don't know, Frank. He goes into the other room of his small flat and returns with some musty publications and diagrams. Makes me study each.

Murder is much the same to me. I was in the Homicide Squad in '64. And by that time I'd done all the things that were there to be done. I was always working on the practical side of police work. And the fresh murders you just went out to them with a group of people, knowing you were going to see something but not be ready for what exactly it is. You have to be ready for any-thing of any kind.

He indicates me to have my coffee. I obey him. His own luncheon is a Four'n'Twenty pie propped on a paper barbecue plate. Stone cold. A fork in it.

That crime could be anything; anything at all. I'm going right back to '40. This bloke had a car and killed someone. We took the body to the mortuary. You took the offender over to the City Watch House and you charged them there. If murder, it's in for them, overnight.

In the murderer Leonski's case, lights were out during the Brownout – you know, during World War II Melbourne's lights were browned out. Two women had been murdered in Melbourne by him, Leonski. I was at Russell Street at the time. Police Headquarters. I lived in the Barracks.

More staring but not for long. He's warming to the subject of locations, arrests and his long service history.

It was very down to earth at the Barracks. You'd eat in an old dingy dining room. Cabbage.

I can smell it now. I love corned beef and cabbage. Steam and in-laws. In that order.

Fortnight dayshift, fortnight nightshift – that's how it was. I was with the Wireless Patrol at the time. It was one-way and they replied in Morse. Morse Code – did I know it? No.

M'first case was the arrest and conviction of a pickpocket. I saw him and just grabbed him. It was straightforward enough, really. I seen him take something off a woman. Got a formal letter from my superintendent about it.

You did what you were told by the officer. Your immediate man was a Two-Striper.

He seems a trifle agitated and tells me he has an appointment to see a specialist in respect of his health. A suspected cancer spot on the cheek. He hands me more books and cuttings and old files, and says we'll see each other soon. I look forward to that.

* * *

When we meet again, Frank Holland wants to tell me the origin of the word larrikin: 'You've been larking around, it means.' He loves origins of meaning. And words. And histories.

'Frank, you've investigated 128 murders. Do any in particular stand out in your memory?'

No.

'But some murders have to be more upsetting than others, surely?'

The Malcolm Wilson shotgun slaying of his wife was pretty savage. The trouble with police these days is that they talk of ethics but just talk a whole lot of bullshit.

Let me quote to you for a moment, a quiet moment, OK? (*He reads from an old pamphlet, mocking the poetic idealism of its hopeful text. He is too realistic for such words.*) 'It's a two-way street. They can't just dump them if they're wrong.' Here's a saying that makes me really laugh, this one. It was found in a cave in 1692 and is supposed to give us a clue as to how to live.

He puts on his glasses and laughs, reading it to me.

'Go placidly ...' What bullshit! It's just a whole lot of blah-blah-blah!

He laughs raucously. I want to read the remainder of that credo but it's put away where I can't possibly see it. I remember it from the Hippie Days.

I served in Cyprus with the peacekeeping forces from the eleventh of May in '64 until the eighth of July of '65. I've done everything. You want to know about the capture and arrest of Ronald Ryan?

We did the Walker–Ryan thing in '65. Caught them in Sydney. Nothing to it. Ryan was just another law-breaker. He was arrested by Ray Kelly and charged at Sydney Central.

Ronald Ryan rang me from Sydney. 'Who's coming up to get me, Mr Holland?'

'How's Ray Kelly going?'

Dead.

I'm not certain how to proceed. Everyone seems to be dead except us two.

Ronald Ryan rang me from Sydney. 'Who's coming up to get me, Mr Holland?' And I told him Ray Kelly.

And that's where our second conversation ended. We had agreed to chat in batches, so as to preserve energy.

When I arrive for the third in the series of attempted interviews with the phlegmatic Holland, I am unfortunately twenty-five minutes late owing to a head gasket problem in my wife's Laser. I press his old-fashioned electric door buzzer and he materialises thirty seconds later like a ghost who never misses a trick. He is alert and brisk at everything, lightning-fast at opening and closing doors and cupboards. I say 'Sorry I'm late, Frank' and he replies bluntly 'I'm sure you are.'

Without waving an arm to indicate that I may sit he speaks of old cases and suggests I read old Police Gazettes to further inquire into the mythology of the police. I may yet.

I gaze for a second or a millisecond at the image of an earlier Holland taken in 1936 with another young policeman. I ask politely who the other fellow might be.

Tresitter.

'His Christian name?'

Oh, bloody hell!

Fair enough. It's a long time ago. Sixty-three years since it was taken.

We drove around after crooks in twelve-cylinder Daimlers. The tyres on them never even squealed or nothing when we tore round corners. They'd clocked 'em at bloody one hundred and five mile an hour on the road. They never had any springs in them. And we sat in the back with the police wireless. Here's a picture. See?

He shoves a magazine at me. There they are, all right, in the old days. It all looks rather scientific with young police listening intently to antiquated radios somewhere.

The operators were in the back. It came over the air. Alertness is everything. We done robbery, the whole lot, everything. There used to be a Shoplifting Squad in the old days, know that?

I didn't, Frank.

Famous crooks back then? Squizzy Taylor was famous. (*He grabs old manilla folder and flips it frantically undone for me.*)
    My last arrest was in 1970. I've won a few commendations. Read that.

And I do, squinting my eyes to follow the old certificate properly. I read out loud the following words to us both: 'For Leadership Displayed In An Investigation'.

Did any murderer appal you, Frank?

'You've asked that.'

I keep reading. Read, read, read. Who's the worst crook you've ever come into contact with?

Bradshaw was a real ratbag, Bradshaw was! Freddie Harrison was pretty bad, too. He was shot dead at a wharf. What's his name shot him. Oh, it'll come to me in a minute. Shot him dead. I've done lots of things. Did peacekeeping duties in Cyprus. We made our name over there by not carrying guns. The chief said to us: 'You're the ones there. You make the decisions. Twelve months we were there.'

It all seems a second ago to this home-made homicide historian.

The Mafia grape murders didn't surprise me. That was always on. Nothing surprises me.
    As to leadership. What's my philosophy on that question, you ask? Well, you're treated as a family. So you listen as one. I used

to say when I was in charge: 'You listen to me. Then give the decision. You'd listen to the lot of 'em. Then they'd say 'Mr Holland said that.' I directed them as to what they should do.

Is it as much a moral conscience as anything else?

Yes, that's right.

No coffee. No drink. Dry words from a dry old cop.

> *You are as a father to the rest. In a sense you are a loving father to them all. In a very real sense, after being involved in the Police Association, I saw myself as their friend and father.*

Conscience comes down from The Top.

As a father, you are as a father to the rest. In a sense you are a loving father to them all. In a very real sense, after being involved in the Police Association, I saw myself as their friend and father. Yes, that's right. Protective. I remember Anne Wregg very well. She was brave and deserved her valour medal. She went to Scotland Yard, deserved to.

'What are criminals like?' Remembers them all, looks up. As if to command them, summon them.

Some crims won't say a word. You put it all to 'em. And lawyers'd say 'Why didn't you put that to my client?' Well, because they wouldn't bloody-well answer when you tried to do just that.

Mostly it was just a matter of how much evidence you put towards them, that's all. John Eric Twist shot Freddie Harrison dead in front of nineteen eye-witnesses down on the dock and no one saw nothing. You work that out.

My three big highlights, you ask? The first obviously was joining up. There were ninety-one of us then. Ninety-one in the whole state of Victoria. Imagine that! Captain Thomas Blamey took us in. He joined the Army later. Here's a picture of all of us in this book here.

'Was your heart pounding when you went in?'

(*He laughs loudly.*) Can't remember that now!

His eyes are twinkling and he suddenly relaxes the old long straight body. It's hard to believe his age. He's youthful and a truthful lovely old bloke.

We went before Selection Boards in the old days. I never made any comparison rules from the old days to now. I was out doing court rounds a lot of the time.

I'll never forget once I brought a fellow in and the old Sarge said 'Never bring anyone else in to make out a report against you, will you, Frank?' He could've been having a piss behind a barrel or something. Something insubstantial, and I've brought him in to make a complaint against me!

Again laughs. Slaps his leg hard. A bit too hard.

You never knock back any citizen who has wandered in to see you. You'd have a sit with them for a minute. If their kid's been shoplifting or something. You warned the kids so their parents'd be glad of it, what you've said to the kids to desist crime, and they'd come in to see you.

Oh, old policeman, you've seen everything and done everything for us. You have your memories intact and manuscripts together for posterity. Thanks for the time to listen to your stories about the old days. You are so brisk, even approaching ninety years of age. Yet you had some time for me, and I thank you. I'm sure there'd be so many people who'd love to meet you.

Above from left to right: Mick Miller and Ray Koch

The late senior constable Ray Koch, 8/4/28–1/6/95

Joined Victoria Police 1949

Retired as senior constable, due to ill-health, 1982

Died 1995

In the course of duty

Jean Koch

Widow of Constable Ray Koch

Twenty years ago Constable Ray Koch was shot twice in the back in his home town of Heathcote. His assailant was the bright-red-bearded Peter Morgan who, with his twin brother, was addicted to 'doing banks'.

Constable Koch survived the gun blasts but after a long convalescence died in 1995.

His widow Jean still lives in this rather dreamy village with bantams asleep on dusty bank window ledges, an ancient public swimming pool, ravenous long-distance truck drivers and no work.

Mrs Koch grew up in the bush and speaks with a crackly country voice reminiscent of fire and sparks on a cold night in the scrub.

She sits quietly in her kitchen with hands firmly grasped. At first she appears self-conscious – and why wouldn't you be, it you were asked to speak of things like the attempted murder of your husband? I wanted to find out about childhood experiences such as bush outings, as well as what it's like to be the wife of a country copper.

Jean has a lusty laugh and fiery temperament, as well as the quietude and contemplativeness to go the distance.

Well, I was born in Bendigo but grew up here in Heathcote. Heathcote, in a word, is home.

I notice a very old set of brass scales resting before the mid-afternoon sun-beams on a kitchen ledge, on them a neat pile of freshly rinsed white rice. Even that sight takes us back.

Heathcote is just somewhere you feel you belong to. I think. My dad came along, too. In January of 1854 my great-grandfather came to Heathcote. He was a great one for the mining. Where did Dad work?

Considers, rests, sighing. Hers is a sweet as well as penetrating bush voice straight out of quartz.

After Dad left school about 1905 he worked at the McIvor Printing Works. He was a reporter for them. Covered meetings and such.

She smiles and blinks. Her teenage grand-daughter Riannin comes in and wanders around. She goes off to buy something up the shops. The house is terribly silent. So is the old road outside. A few kids off to the local swimming-pool, laughing.

Where the Heathcote Police Station is now – I did my schooling there. You go up that way through the hills. The range you might have noticed when you came in is part of the Great Dividing Range. Rabbiting. We used to love rabbiting! Mum'd cut lunch for us. One of the friends was one or two year old when we all went rabbiting. You'd walk out three or four miles or more. Lift the pram over the fence – that baby went rabbiting with you.

She is like the happy bush girl again.

Nets and ferrets! If you ran out of nets you stood there with your hands over the hole. You had to be quick. You saw the bunny coming out of the burra and you'd just grab it quick by its head and wring its neck. Ha! Ha!

She makes a loud squish sound and laughs.

Gut them with your favourite knife. You gut it and hook the hind legs together. Cut between the sinew and the bone. On a good day you'd get twenty or thirty-odd. The place was lousy with rabbits. They'd all get hooked up in the net. It was just good fun, rabbiting.

She looks away into country-space, resting her right hand under her sun-browned chin. She is very lined with age but at sixty-nine she looks pretty fit, with eagerness.

Wild Duck Creek was where we rabbited. You can walk up to the Viewing Rock just up the range there. You'd ride to Pyalong or out to Mia Mia. I was full of go when I was young.

She undoes a can of cigarette tobacco and offers it to me, but I politely decline the generous offer. She rolls one for herself and puffs thickly – satisfied. A long, hard drag on it. Squints to the left eye. Stares straight at me.

Not so long back, I wrote a lot of my stories for our daughter, the eldest one, Lyn Elsbury. (She had to interview someone who'd lived through the Depression times for her kindergarten teaching certificate. She's the brainy one of the family. Got her Bachelor of Education certificate.) December 26, 1930 was when I was born. I was writing all this past-stuff out for a couple of months.

As kids we were very close but you never had much. Dad had a few sheep, a few fruit trees, a country garden. Mum did preserved fruit bottling. Life around here didn't really come good until about 1939. And then there was a war!

Laughs. Bangs fist hard down on little table.

Dad had a foot-operated lathe. A steam-engine train with Nugget Shoe Polish lids for wheels. He'd make you a home-made train, sorta thing. You'd get something like that for Christmas or your birthday present and you thought that was pretty good.

You sat at the table and you had what was put in front of you. If you declined it you had it again the next night. If we had an excess of anything like fruit or vegetables or whatever it was, we shared it with our friends, the neighbours, in the old times. They'd often have something you didn't have growing, so you swapped.

Wish those times would come back for city folk. We've got what's called 'Blockies' up here. They're the city people who don't share. They come up here from the Big Smoke but never talk to the ones born here. They think they're better than you at first. Then they go on the dole – and then everyone's equal!

When real estate people show them through, they take them to look at a green patch in the winter and it all seems nice. But it's only onion weed and it soon goes brown in next-to no time and the stock won't eat it. Real estate people dupe the city ones so easily.

She stares down as though searching for answers as to why this is so. But life is awful in many ways, and some answers don't. She bites her lips.

We get some of the Blockies at the Heathcote Ambulance Op Shop, where I work. They come in there for a fifty-cent shirt, and I'm glad to sell it to them. We sell clothing, you know. Odds and ends and bits and pieces from five cents to six dollars. You can buy a full men's suit for only $16. Dresses are only $1 to $12. And we've done really well. We've been going for sixteen years and we've got the best equipped two ambulances in the State. Paid fully off!

A look of triumph. As if to say 'Could you do better?' I could not.

We've got about twenty girls. All voluntary. Some do a couple of days a week – nine till four.

I can see them there, snowy-haired, violet-permed. Friendly old country mums. Backbone of our nation. Unstoppable. Tiny, tough and tall.

We took in $20,000 dollars in the 1998–99 financial year alone! That worked out at $18,800 profit after rent, gas and electricity. We have a very clear philosophy at our shop: if you can get twenty cents for something, you're better off selling it.

'What's it like in Heathcote?'

Drugs and unemployment. Some have been seen using heroin in the Bush. (*As though a witness is seeing a junkie shooting up behind wattle.*) You do see needles, syringes, around the town. A lot of young people are on the Dole. There's nothing to do. They smoke, drink, smoke, drink.

She looks at me with a 'What's going on in our country?' look. Then folds her cardigan'd arms. She's pragmatic, resigned.

I was fifteen when I left school. It's called Year Nine, now. Our old school used to be where the police station is. It was State School number 300. Left school here in '39. You were supposed to leave your school and make Army uniforms. I learnt hat-making from Mrs Lewis. Her husband come from round here. She bought the florist shop next to her. And I learnt floristry from her. I wanted to do dressmaking. So I learnt hemming and hand-made button-holes – double thread right round. I could sew without glasses. We did mattress covers until the work ran out. I went to Pelaco after the war finished. This is '47, '48-ish. A good coupla years. Went to Roebex Leather after that. Only twenty or so worked there – just as noisy as Pelaco. (*She holds her ears in remembrance of vast clattering and deafening garment machines.*)

I'd known Ray for ages, since he was eighteen. He was born in Colbinabbin. You go on from Heathcote, up the Elmore Road. He played for Colbinabbin. Footy in the Heathcote League. Ruck mostly. I sort of met him at a cuppla dances.

'What were those bush dances like?'

They were at St Killian's Hall, next door to the church – a 50–50 sorta thing. You did the foxtrot. The good thing about dancing the progressive barn dance was that you could catch up with gossip with all your new partners. You got up and danced and you chatted in relay. You could chat and laugh with everyone in the district. That's how you got the news.

Ray wasn't too bad a dancer. I didn't go to dances until I was sixteen. I was breaking my neck to go to dances. There was a school ball every year. A fancy dress ball, always! Kids'd dance from half-past seven until nine. Then they'd have supper – then it was the parents' turn to dance. Real normal fun dances it was. Hand round supper: sandwiches and cream cakes, all home-made.

Big sigh. Big gulping sigh for what once was but is no longer. She means innocent bush fun is gone. Everyone's got tough. Or weak.

The kids of today, they want drink or they don't want to know about it. Young kids of today say 'There's nothing to do round the place.'

I saw a few kids on my way into town. Staring at tar on the main drag.

'We want something to do of a night-time,' they say. Like a club. But the kids want to bring drink. Drink's become a contagion in the Bush.

I waltz Jean back to her early memories of Ray, and ask her what sort of a background he was from.

One brother, he had, and three sisters. His old man was George. Tough. He was tall, aroundabout five foot ten, fifteen stone – thick-set like Ray was. As a teenager, Ray did seasonal work – things like cropping and ploughing. He done road work with The Shire up there. He used to drive the trucks in the backyards. He was a real happy-go-lucky man at the beginning. He used to say to me in his country sorta voice: 'Hurry up will you? You talk too slowly!'

But not today. Her mind is swift but not racing. She enjoys talking and is god at it, I must say.

He went into the Force cozza the job security. As good a reason, I think, as any other one. In '49 he entered, I think. It's a long time ago now. Hang on, look at this. There's his certificate. In fact, there's a couple. His dates are 19/7/49 to 29/4/82. He is Raymond George Koch.

She stares at a few certificates, including one that is framed. There's no sound, not even sounds of breezes or any football being kicked out on the footpath. Quite quiet.

His first police station was Fitzroy. He lived in the barracks at Russell Street, then went to work from there. He was happy boarding at the barracks.

Was that similar to boarding on the convict hulks?

It wasn't that bad! Hot meals were made for you and you ate in a communal dining-room. He did his washing and cleaning like everyone else. (*She claps her hands with a big smack.*) He washed his favourite white cricket jumper in the copper once! Boiled it in the copper so it just came out a big yukky mess!

He was a constable at Fitzroy. Then he went to Toorak Police Station in '51. We were married here at Heathcote, in '51, at the Presbyterian Church. It's not here any more. There's only private movies there now. That's what they show there.

Nothing whatever from the past seems long ago any more. Quite the contrary. Birds sing in the present tense from the road. Birds love only the present. The past eludes them.

We had our honeymoon at Lakes Entrance after our wedding. We got the train to Sale – six hours, it took. Never got there till nearly midnight. 'Have you got any idea where we can get a room at the pub?' Ray had said to his superiors. They said 'We've got a cheap sleepout at Neil Shuey's place. His son is assistant commissioner.' The bungalow was all right.

We went from Sale to Lakes Entrance next day. At midnight the owner knocked. 'The Boss wants you. The fellows at Toorak Police Station said that house you wanted, the one you was keen on that you could live in comfortably, you've got it! You've got to come back to work.' They did that as a joke. One of the old blokes we knew used to say that kind of house they build by the mile and chop them up as they go along. But it would've been so close to Ray's work. It would've been handy – within walking distance – because he didn't have a car in those days. Before we were married we got round together on Matchless 500 motorbike. I've been 120 mile an hour on the back of it, hanging on to him.

Ray was a policeman from Toorak to Camperdown. All over. He was seven years there. He had a shift to Portland. If there was no house gazetted you didn't go. You had to get a house with the police station if you had kids.

These little police stations didn't have cars with them so the cars the police used in tiny country towns were their own ones. They drove their own cars to make arrests or transport prisoners.

I was expecting our second son, Peter. So I said 'He can bloody-well go on his own!' I stayed till I had Peter. The week I came out of hospital, Ray had been down there three months. He'd been relieving all round the district. Heathcote came vacant when they made it into a two-man station. There was no house with it. Lived with my dad, we all did.

'What were Ray's duties?'

General duties of their station was his job. Office work. Summonses. Interviewing anyone if there was any crime. These little police stations didn't have cars with them so the cars the police used in tiny country towns were their own ones. They drove their own cars to make arrests or transport prisoners. We bought a car in Camperdown in '52. It was a Vauxhall.

I pictured country cops choofing around collecting criminals hiding out in barns and irrigation channels – lying low, as they say in the movies – and then the steadfast policemen inserting the criminals into old dark green Morris Minors capable of sixty flat chat. Jump-starting them.

Ray's best mates were from round here. He was good at keeping his mates, he kept friends from long ago. They hailed from way back, from his schooldays and that. One special chap from Colbinabbin was John West – he'd make the effort to go and see him. They'd sit together and have a yarn. He was best man at our wedding.

She sips coffee and puts out her smoke. Grinds it out bluntly. Ah!

'Once a policeman, always a policeman', the old saying is right. Ray couldn't let his restless mind go. Always reacting like a good copper. He and me'd be out walking and he'd notice things all the time. 'There's tyres in that driveway and they don't use that driveway. It's a short wheelbase – you know, a different car.' Me, I'd go past and wouldn't see it.

She is so alert. Quick like a bush bird, she darts into the past.

'Well, back in the job at that stage a lot of copper wiring was being pinched around Heathcote. And this car come through and Ray noticed the back was real low. So he says to the darkened driver: 'What's in the boot?'

'I got a cod in there,' the driver says, sinking lower into the front seat.

'Oh, yeah?' says Ray. 'Give us a look.'

Opens it up and it's copper wire. No cod is going to make it that low.

This was in the late '60s, when he was so well. He's been gone more than four years now. He died on the first of June in '94. In '82 he was out of the job. He used up his sick leave. He was a policeman here for twenty-one years.

His weight'd go up to nineteen stone. It'd fluctuate. Up and down he went, healthwise, weightwise. He done miles and miles of fox hunting. He skun the foxes himself. Keen fisherman. Good sense of humour – said you need it. His irritability'd crop up a bit. But he could sleep at the drop of a hat.

She says he used to come home from work and take a nap on the couch at lunchtime, out like a light, straight away. One minute you're talking to him then he's conked.

He was always early to sleep of a night-time. Then half past six or seven in the morning he'd drive the car half a mile to work.

This is before we were living behind the Heathcote Police Station.

He was shot in '79. At the side of the National Bank in Barak Street. That's where the bush was that Ray saw Morgan behind. It was the third time it'd been robbed by Peter Morgan. The Morgan robbers were identical twins with incredible red hair and beards. While Ray was in hospital, I got threatening letters. It was hard to believe threatening mail could come to our home at a time like that when Ray was so sick.

She plonks some hot water into our coffee mugs and continues grimly. Pours glumly. Sips slowly.

I'd gone to the Base Hospital at Bendigo to see Ray – that's where he was admitted. It was about half past four on a Friday. I could hear a rush of feet. 'Did you see that fellow standing there?' said someone. 'Just standing there to the left of the lift.'

The thief Morgan, he only used to do it in the wintertime. Robberies. Wintertime robberies, it was. He was pretty scared of snakes in the summertime.

We thought immediately it must've been one of the twins. But it was just some innocent bystander who said afterwards 'The beard's comin' orf as soon as I get home!' He was just over from Bendigo, the man who was standing by the hospital lift. He was waiting to see his wife who was having a baby.

She rolls her eyes to show 'Poor bloke.'

The thief Morgan, he only used to do it in the wintertime. Robberies. Wintertime robberies, it was. He was pretty scared of snakes in the summertime. He had a motorbike on the Showground Road. Nobody knew which robber was which as they were identical. He'd been up in the showgrounds – a kid said he'd seen him there.

On the day it happened, the State Savings Bank manager came over and said 'We've been told there's going to be a hold-up today.' Ray did a tour of Heathcote, just having a drive around. He saw someone standing in a shrub – or something, at least, in a shrub. It was Morgan in Barak Street. He stepped out from behind that shrub, with the gun on Ray.

She acts out this deed physically.

Ray used to say 'If you're ever faced with a gun, don't make a grab for it!' And then he did just that: made a grab for it. Morgan was left-handed so he had to pass the gun from his left to right hand to work it because the safety catch must have been on.

It went off. Ray got up again and went to roll away. Morgan is standing over him. Ray's on his stomach. Morgan fired a shot into Ray's back. And Ray said that really hurt him. He was so bad Morgan had to help Ray into the bank he was robbing. Assist him. The bank was quiet at the time.

Morgan made Ray sit there on that same seat Ray always sat on when he went to do his own banking. Isn't it ironic. Ray was so bad Morgan said to the bank chappie 'You'd better get him an ambulance.'

It was more or less attempted murder. I was at home and I didn't know anything about it. It would've been about quarter to five. Shirl from the newsagency said there had been an accident.

The bank teller said back 'Well, what's the phone number?' We'd just changed over from manual exchange to automatic.

And Morgan said back 'How the hell would I know?', while Ray's just sitting there groaning after being shot. Then Gordon Walker, who was out in the backyard of the newsagent's, said 'I've just heard a couple of rifle shots. And Barb went over to see what could be done. With the second shot, a local priest, Frank Marriott, came over to see what he could do to help.

It was more or less attempted murder. I was at home and I didn't know anything about it. It would've been about quarter to five. And Barb said 'We'd better go and tell Jean, because someone might just drop over to their home and ask 'How's Ray?''

She rolls her eyes sarcastically. Like 'How would that be?'

It's Friday afternoon. Just gone five o'clock. You can imagine the traffic on the highway to Bendigo Hospital. It's absolutely horrendous. Our son Pete had a panel van then, and he was taking me in to see Ray. He's got the lights flashin' and the horn blowin'. This is our son driving. I was numb – almost no feeling on the way.

My son pulled us up at Bendigo Hospital. *She gets up to mime wonky, wobbly legs: just about the only time she's stood up.* My legs are going like that! Peter was all right. He can take anything, like. He's pretty sort of with it in an emergency.

Ray said, 'It's no good giving me the last rites because I'm not going to die.'

Before they put the tube down his neck, they said 'We've only found one bullet!' This was in the operating theatre. I was talking to him just before he went under.

She looks shocked. Her eyes are enormous. Staring at me, incredulous.

Ray said 'I've shot enough rabbits to know there are two bullets in me. There's got to be a hole.' One bullet had gone in and out again. They thought it was the only one fired.

So they're looking for it. Morgan's shot Ray twice, actually. Twice! Both bullets must've stayed in him. Ray said if the bullet had come out, the skin would've been forced outwards, not inwards. In Bendigo they could only find one bullet. But a second one was found at St Vincent's.

We buzzed back home and grabbed some clothing. 'He's not too good,' they said, after that.

When he was on the run after the robbery Morgan was seen by Rick Hastie, a policeman, in Pall Mall in Bendigo. Hastie says to Morgan 'What's in the case?'

He chased Morgan into a laneway. He then had to open that case up. Rick straightened up and Morgan stuck the gun into the middle of Rick's gut. He then pulled the trigger and it just went 'click'.

All that money was in a blue bag inside that case. And Rick has thought 'He's got it on the safety, so it can't go off.'

See, Morgan was left-handed. Right-handed guns were awkward for him. Rick just grabbed him. He says 'Tell them over at the police station I've got the guy who shot Ray Koch!'

Ray had bad internal bleeding. Seventeen holes, they patched up. On the Saturday morning they opened him up and all his veins were bleeding. He could feel it all filling him up, all the blood.

The bullet had gone into his heart. It'd been shot into the main vein, you know, the artery. It had a sort of voyage into his heart, Ray's heart, my husband's heart.

He was in Bendigo Hospital three weeks. I used to go to see him each day because I was in Bendigo. You'd go in and wonder if he's going to get over it. He was only conscious occasionally. They done open heart on him after that at St Vincent's. They stuck this breathing thing out of his neck so he could breathe and that. That was in for a week and a half.

They X-rayed him at St Vincent's. The bullet had gone into his heart. It'd been shot into the main vein, you know, the artery. It had a sort of voyage into his heart, Ray's heart, my husband's heart.

She sits motionless now and there's still no noise whatever. She has ceased talking and gulps. Big ones they are.

I've got them here, both of them, the bullets, if you'd like to see them. Two of them. Thirty-twos.

She ventures into the spare room and returns smartly with a bizarre perspex orb containing two bullets the police gave her as a souvenir. She peers into it. I notice one bullet is completely bent in half.

He was six and a half weeks all told in hospital. And two weeks in Melbourne.

Something happened there, too. I turned up with my cousin and the Sister said 'Who are you?' You're not allowed to bring in extra visitors.' Then I saw a policeman standing there. I asked Ray what was going on.

He was in this big ward and a chap had come into the ward and whispered to Ray, 'Do you remember me?'

Ray couldn't remember him and the man said to Ray 'It's a pity you weren't killed.' It was a chap Ray had arrested in Fitzroy years before.

Her eyes say 'People are great, aren't they?' But she laughs with a careless contempt. She's seen everything that life can hurl at you. And a lot more.

He was a JP and a drunk, in that order, that chap who sneered that to Ray. Ray had had to go to court over arresting that man for drunkenness in Fitzroy years before, and the chap has said 'I'll get you for this.' So Ray grabbed him by the ankles and pulled him back to the police station. Ray was fined five pounds for that, but the drunk was only fined four pounds. He turned out to be the same chap who sent Ray the threatening letters.

She looks into the orb of discharged bullets once again; me too. They are small things, of brass. All broken up.

Ray was pretty lousy when they brought him back home again. Come home, he did, in his summer pyjamas. He said it felt like a ten-mile walk to the toilet. What a trudge.

He would've come down to about fourteen stone from sixteen. He wasn't too bad at night. But if he was sitting down alone, just sitting down alone watchin' the telly or something on his own, if you snuck up on him he just about died, sorta thing. He'd jump straight up in the air in shock.

Ray had a shotgun loaded by the front door and by the back door and he carried a Browning Automatic. He was becoming really frightened all the time.

The other twin had escaped from jail. I forget his first name now. It'll come to me. He wasn't considered dangerous, but that didn't console Ray. He was nervy all the time. He'd go right off the planet. He was real paranoid. A lot! He went back to Heathcote Police Station to do light duties but he couldn't even handle those. That was eighteen months before we moved to this house. I'd say it's no good getting upset but Ray thought the brother was coming for him.

She looks blank. Is life blank now? She's making the best of it, I'd say. She won't submit to anything, Jean. Fearless bush copper's widow.

Of a summertime on a hot day he'd sit round havin' cold stubbies. He'd get to a 'Ha, Ha' stage. He had a good sense of humour in the beginning, but he'd get real nasty in the end. He saw a shrink about it. He said 'I'm not going back there any more. You just go over and over and over it all the time. It's on your mind constantly.' He was born in '28. He was fifty-three when it happened. Here are his commendations.

'I shouldn't've made a grab for that gun,' he used to often say. Over and over he said that, in regret. 'Why did I go for his gun?'

We look at Ray's awards for courage. They seem empty things without him around. But she's proud of them, I suppose.

He got the Queen's Commendation for Brave Conduct and the Good Conduct Medal. He got a letter from Margaret Thatcher and laurel leaves from the Queen when she was in Melbourne. I said 'They'd make nice earrings.'

He just moped round after that. He'd read the paper from front to back. Had lots of time to kill. Sit in the sun in the morning. He had two Foxies up on his knee. They were his little boys. 'I shouldn't've made a grab for that gun,' he used to often say. Over and over he said that, in regret. 'Why did I go for his gun?'

You say the saying all your working life and then you don't listen to it. In the finish, like, it was a relief. He had cirrhosis of the liver. He give up drink once for a couple of years. But coming on Christmas time out would come the stubbies. He died on the first of June of 1995.

He was sick all the time. In and out of hospital. The doctor said he wanted to see us. 'Two months to live' is what they said. That sort of flattened him, Ray.

He had Hep C. That combined with the liver killed him in the end. He had thirty-two pints of blood put through him when he went in. He was yellow some days. Some not. I used to come home and that and find him sitting there crying. He was not philosophical about it, getting shot. He used to say 'Why's this happened to me?' sort-a-thing. In the finish he'd be on a walking-stick to get around – he'd be pretty shaky and he wouldn't have anyone help him or anything. He'd say 'Get away or I'll hit you with the walking-stick!'

Now you think it's a shocking thing to happen to a good country copper. I'm never scared of anything actually. I knew Morgan wouldn't come around.

She just trails off and it's time for me to go. If good police have heart, she's their soul.

The late constable Garry Holmes, 14/3/60–21/7/96

Joined Victoria Police 1994

Died 1996

'Don't worry about me'

Leeanne Holmes

Widow of Constable Garry Holmes

The kids are at school when Leeanne Holmes, thirty-nine, meets me at a country railway station as arranged. Clouds float overhead like fluffy malted milks as she drives me from here to her bright and hopeful house, where her brother-in-law, Graham, is doing a bit of gardening out the front. It's so sunny and temperate today.

Mrs Holmes lost her husband, Constable Garry Holmes, three and half years ago in a drunk driver hit-and-run accident. His photograph now grins down at us from one wall.

How does it feel to be a police widow? Filleted, I imagine, like any other widow or widower. But can we really know how the heart feels after such a senseless incident that happens in the course of duty or on the way to the job?

The home is full of flowers and Mrs Holmes looks curious, understandably; restrained. She looks at me with apprehension and concern. Like what do you want? But friendly too.

I can see her neighbours carrying fresh dirt in wheelbarrows and watering their new plants. It's a new suburb – what's called an estate. It is pleasant enough. The Dandenongs shimmer bluely in middle distance. It's hazy.

'To begin with could you please tell me, Leeanne, about life in your twenties?'

We did nightclub things back then, when I was so young, you know. Out here in Ferntree Gully there are pubs. The Middle Hotel is where you went. Bouncers. Late nights. I liked being married.

'When did you first meet Garry?'

I first met Garry when I was working in Knox. He was a store-man at that time, at a place called Dynavac. We were married in 1990, on the sixth of May. He's actually English.

We look up at his smiling photo. Seems like a nice guy.

He was amusing without really trying, you know? He was very, very easy-going. He was a hassle-free sort of guy. He was really my best friend. He was a very good listener. No sulking! Always happy. He had this sort of a face that always smiled. He was very strongly family-minded. He always believed the family came first – that old people in particular should be looked after, that we, as younger citizens, should look after the oldies. He was a relief to be with.

She falls silent upon this, as you'd expect. She leans her bright face on her hand to remember.

I really looked forward to seeing him come home to me at the end of every day.

'Why did Garry join the police force?' I wonder aloud.

He had wanted to be a policeman when he was younger. He was trying hard to grow to be six foot tall because you had to be six foot then when you went in. So he just had to wait. (*Laughs.*)

He sat the entrance exam but failed the essay. He passed everything else. Then he did the preparatory course, in essays. He made certain he'd pass it next time. Pure determination, he was! It's hard, you know, the essay exam, because the topic is unknown to you at the time: it could be about anything. It's a two-day thing, the entrance exam. You go in one day and do the maths. Then you do the physical – the swimming and the obstacle course.

The next intake, he passed. He got it in the maths. Did an interview with the Board. Had a month to go until the Academy. That's how he found out he passed. He didn't have to sweat it out going to the letterbox each day.

She shifts forward in her chair, stirring the coffee, and her voice is not really so relaxed. Careful. Speaking slowly.

We've got four children. The youngest, one of two boys, was only two years old when Garry died, so he'll never know him as the father he should have. The girls would've been eleven and twelve at the time.

'Was there a significant drop in pay when he went into the Police Academy?'

The police pay at the Academy was much worse than at his old storeman's job. Garry dropped ten thousand a year to be a copper. It was for that reason that he felt nervous, you know, giving up his old job. There were just so many things he always wanted to do. He'd say 'It's now or never.'

   He rang me every night. He felt very nervous about that side of things, ringing up when he slept at the Academy. He was always reliably prompt, right on time. When you stay at the Academy you have to pay board but if you're married you don't have to, so that's one good thing.

It's easy to talk and hard to talk. Better to talk.

He slept there for five months, would come home on the weekends. After the first Friday night, when he came home, he burst into tears. They'd really put the cadets through a lot. A lot of, you know, heavy teasing. He was just so happy to be home.

'Did you celebrate the temporary home coming?'

It was a celebration. Yes, of course it was. I can see him standing at the entrance to his own home. There was a lot of hard work for him to get through and get done. A lot to learn. Exams, it was hard work! Every night he did homework there.

'How did you get by? Money must have been tight? Was everything carefully budgeted?'

I actually did family day care for the Shire. I did that in our own home, looking after kids. Garry's pay went into the Police Credit Co-Op.

Garry made a terrific friend at the Academy. Scott James, his name is. Scott's wife had a baby and my husband became the godfather. He got lonely for me and the kids. He'd say 'The Law's too hard.' Or 'I'd better go back to my old storeman's job.' But his old squad took him running, and he loved it out there. He was just so dedicated.

'Where was he first stationed?'

Hastings. He was a constable there – in 1994, I think. He was there for four or five months. Then they sent him to Chelsea because he was only a trainee. I can remember him having to do everything: sit in the car for hours doing surveillance work, check boats for seaworthiness, direct traffic, go off to domestics. There was one case where the wife had locked the husband out, and the police had to go and calm him down. Another time, some girl at Hastings got drunk and started causing a scene, running down the street with her dressing-gown wide open.

Usually, when he did a night shift, it was about seven or eight in the morning when he came home. He'd be very wound up. Like a purge it was, sitting there with a cup of tea and me listening. He went to one house when the husband had died at home, in his forties. That's all he was – forty years old – and that whole family just sitting there. It was the condition of the kids, having to see the body, that was really hard.

Garry was good at counselling people. One of the police-women from Chelsea, Naomi, told me after Garry had died that he was just so good with teenagers. He didn't speak to them from a lofty height; he spoke to them in their own language. He never, ever said anything like 'I'm the cop!' He spoke to them as an equal. He didn't show off just because of his uniform. Naomi really liked him. She's stayed in touch. The sympathy and understanding still coming from her are outstanding. She's done follow-up. I see a few of them; not a lot.

'What sort of hours did he normally work?'

His shift was the normal eight hours. Sometimes in the night, I'd wake up and he wouldn't be home. If he was stuck in court he wouldn't be able to ring me. They'd go on, those cases, until four or five or six in the morning.

> *I knew, if he didn't ring, that he couldn't ring ... He used to say 'Look, don't worry about me.' But you do.*

Long are the hours, long. And the silence at home is that way, too. It's lonely for policemen's wives. Life is unpredictable.

I knew, if he didn't ring, that he *couldn't* ring – I knew that. He just couldn't and you had to accept it. He used to say 'Look, don't worry about me.' But you do. You do worry about them. I was just paranoid about it.

The day he died he was due to start at 7 am. They rang because he wasn't there. And I could hear a guy in the background say 'Stop that call.'

Garry could see trouble on that road – that bloody Thompsons Road, Cranbourne! He really hated going on it. He said to me not long before he died, 'I want to get a job at Warragul and go on a safer road.' It's ironic that he died on a road he hated because it's not safe.

*He was just driving to work. Left home at ten past six –
on the Sunday morning, it was ... Had his uniform on.*

He died at 6.25 am. He was just driving to work. Left home at ten past six – on the Sunday morning, it was. July 21st, 1996. Had his uniform on. He hadn't even had breakfast. Garry didn't have breakfast as a rule. Just a cup of tea and off to work.

'What kind of driver hit your husband?'

He was .186 blood alcohol on the wrong side of the road. He was just drunk and ran straight into Garry.

Garry died instantly. He braked and the front of the car went down and the big heavy car that hit him went up and straight through. The drunk's car was on the wrong side of the road and went straight through him. Garry braked but there was nowhere to go.

He would've been a vegetable if he'd lived through it. His legs were crushed and everything was smashed up. And he only had one week to go till his training was finished. He'd just finished his final exam.

'How were you told, Leanne?'

A knock came at the door and I saw a police car out the front, through our window. So I thought 'Garry's home.' One man at the door said 'I'm Garry's boss. Garry's been involved in a car accident and he has died.' I just about fell on the floor... I was in shock. It was unreal, the whole thing. I said to Garry's boss, 'This is a joke. This isn't happening to me! He's only thirty-six.'

They then asked me to give them the names and phone numbers of Garry's family.

Police Legacy were wonderful – still are – to us. Senior police from quite high-up came to our home when the accident first happeneds – Inspectors, Chief Inspectors. Not just phoning, but making the effort to come out here and see me properly, one to one, person to person.

I didn't eat for days after Garry died. Couldn't. Just shock. But you can't just fold up. (*Makes a fold-up or collapsing action with her hands in front of her to demonstrate.*)

They told me they were sorry, but they would look after us. They told me about my entitlements. They arranged for me to see an accountant. I had no money worries.

When Garry died he was in the middle of building a picket fence. So the police from Chelsea (where he was stationed) held a working bee, at my house. They finished building it. They said it was something they wanted to do for Garry.

'And the children?'

With kids you just want to die, yourself, but you keep on going.

The littlest child, he couldn't take it in. Even now, every night he says 'I love you, Mummy! I love you, Daddy!' but he doesn't really know who Daddy is. One of the boys still cries about it.

With kids you just want to die, yourself, but you keep on going. The kids have to have clean clothes, I've got to get them off to school, see to their activities. My mother stayed with us for a short while, but after a few weeks she had to go home, too. My sister from Queensland came down at the time but she, too, had to go home because she's got her own family.

Face up and eyes up, you have to face life.

The garden needed doing. Garry's brother has been great. The friendship I've got with my dead husband's brother keeps my husband's memory alive.

Garry's mother's just devastated. His father's still alive. They had the funeral at the Academy.

'What happened to the drunk driver?'

This bloody drunken guy only got a few bruises – he basically only went to hospital for observation. He got five years with a minimum of three.

Her open face shows a hiss of contempt.

He was a tyre-fitter – been out all Saturday night, boozing in Frankston, then decided to drive back to his place. He's shown no remorse whatsoever – doesn't believe in his guiltiness. Even his mother got up in court and the barrister said 'Are you sorry or remorseful for what he's done?' And she said 'No.'

Last November he went to prison. There's been no letter of apology. He was twenty-six when it happened. If I killed someone because I'd been drinking, I'd feel sick at what I'd done. You're told and told and told not to drink and drive, and they still do it. Even his mother hasn't written anything to me. It's been three and a half years, now.

I got a letter from Neil Comrie, showing sympathy. My best friend from school, Carol, who lives in Berwick now, was there for me when Garry died.

But my lasting feeling is that I just feel sorry for Garry, I really feel sorry for him. He was a wonderful father and he was so patient with everything, not just the children and myself.

Outside we step into the optimistic old sun and wander through flowerbeds and I have a last squint at the Dandenongs through that friendly blue haze, with people driving everywhere and doing all kinds of things. Having their family dinners soon, laughing together – those with families, that is.

From left to right: Jimmy Skilling and Ralph West

Ralph West

Member of the Victoria Police 1956–85

You need to be able to laugh

Ralph West – retired police officer, aged 72

In my conversation with Colleen Woolley it emerged I should chat with veteran policeman Ralph West. He'd been on the motorbikes as well as lectured to motorcycle police in his capacity as public relations officer. He'd also done the hard yards, both as long-serving counsellor for distraught parents in times of fatal car smashes and on call during savage bushfires in the Dandenong Ranges.

When I turned up at Ralph's Doncaster home I was greeted by a cheerful senior citizen in a musky lime cardigan with scrolly buttons all down the front and an immaculate grin that shone in the blotchy afternoon sunshine of his front porch.

Inside, his wife Joy welcomed me warmly before an impressive collection of teaspoons from all over the earth and offered me coffee. The home was so tranquil and filled with purpose that it was impossible to imagine trouble of any kind.

Ralph curled up in his easychair with panache and folded his hands together like a cane basket. He's balding, tall with a slightly curved spine and large inquiring eyes that are dark and bright simultaneously. He has a working face filled with interest and unstoppable zest. But on this occasion it is his sharp-as-a-pin power of access to his policing past that interests me most.

You go into the Police, I suppose, because you hope you can make a difference. It works off hopes I suppose. I joined in '56. St Kilda Road Depot.

The sun streams through the sitting room and Ralph West fiddles with a brightly coloured tie. He's hard to read. Tense and easygoing at the same time. Tough. Nice. Avuncular.

During the Depression years we weren't that well off and, by Gee, kids can be cruel! I remember that some were very cruel and they used to sing out insults at us if we looked poorer. I came home from Sunday School crying because of some of their comments.

Patches on ya pants, that sorta thing, that's what they'd joke at! Kids sling off at things like that. But I can remember pleasant Sunday afternoons, too. Those were my days as a 'Metho': a member of the West Preston Methodist Church. I played cricket for South Preston Methodist Church. That's a few year ago now. I was a baby in Northcote, grew up in Preston. In my younger years, Mum and Dad took me to Wesley Church in Lonsdale Street, where Doctor C. Irving Benson was the minister. In those days the gents had a suit and tie and ladies wore hat, gloves and handbag. (*As though there can be no other form of lady.*)

He is stiller now and Joy sits in the corner, occasionally chuckling and throwing in a few quips in a friendly voice, but leaving the reminiscing to Ralph.

We'd go to Wesley to worship in Dad's 1927 Rugby car! It was an old tourer, that car! Mum had a simple faith: 'Just trust in the Lord.' We were not a great religious family. 'Do unto others' was our motto. Mum'd say that to us and that would be it.

Mum's Christianity was practical. If those around you had nothing, you had nothing. I watched Sean Connery on the telly the other night and he came from unbelievable poverty. He never thought about it. In our day, when we were poor and starting out, we never saw any people starving. Things were shared around. If someone made some jam, it was passed around, door to door, mouth to mouth. It's only now that I appreciate my Christian upbringing.

Dad was Mum's confidanté. He was in France during the First World War. He said once 'You can never wash away problems through the bottom of a bottle.'

Quite right. I sip my coffee with unbridled relish. Ralph is indefatigable. He is out every other evening, giving talks. In fact, he's so active, running about everywhere giving talks and going to police dinners and fund-raisers, that I feel lucky to have caught him at home.

They come over from Norwich, England, in 1922, my lot. One sister – Joan. My Dad worked at Tilbury's – a cabinet-making factory in Collingwood. He left and got a job as a property renovator just before the Second World War broke out. He was conscripted into the Civil Construction Corps. He went up to Queensland to build Army camps and accommodations – huts and so on. My father was a Jack-of-all-trades, master-of-none, kinda thing. He helped build the Great Ocean Road with a pick and a shovel during the Depression years.

We speak of Ralph's schooling – a subject he is obviously comfortable with. He is the eternal schoolboy.

I only had two schools: South Preston State and Preston Tech. I wasn't a great reader. You used to have to make your own fun outside. At Bradford's paddock there was a lovely old Mulberry tree good to climb. At school, one of the games we used to play was called Cherry Bobs.

'I sort of remember that. How is it played again?'

The one who conducted the game would dig a small hole in the ground and straddle it. You had to try to cast your cherry 'bob' into the shallow. (Cherry pips, also known as cherry 'bobs', were improvised marbles.) And if your cherry bob stayed in there you got two-to-one in gambling terms. Or you got three-to-one, depending on the degree of difficulty. You were betting with cherry pips. It was a breeding ground for SP bookies.

He mimes firing a cherry pip and squints one eye, like Huckleberry Finn all of a sudden.

We played another game called Tip-Tap, using two pieces of wood. It was a popular home-made entertainment during the Depression. Fun was free, so you had plenty of it. There were paddocks everywhere, not like the recreational parks of today. These were open paddocks, open to everyone.

He stretches his long legs and wriggles his feet. Brown slacks and terribly neat. No clocks tick in this peaceful atmosphere, yet there's an energy in the quiet. The energy of memory.

I often wonder what's happened to the old scallywag school. People are so serious these days. I think you need a bit of fun. You really need laughter to cope with life. You have your grief for friends shifting away to another suburb. Or your dog dies and you go under.

This old policeman hasn't gone under and you get the impression that he hasn't changed one iota since he was born. He is a larrikin realist, like any natural child.

Did I love the community? I loved going to the Preston Market. Mum did two days a week at the old Preston Market in Plenty

Road – she worked at a fruit and veg stall kinda thing. She was a menace to go up the street with. Wherever she went Mum'd bump into people. She had an affinity with people. She'd sit in bus stops and have conversations with anyone she met.

'Did you do any sort of work before you joined the Force?'

Yeah, I wanted to be a mechanic in '42. As a youngster I got a job at the Canada Cycle and Motor Company on the corner of Queen and A'Beckett streets. A large, two-storeyed building with car ramps down to the workshops and one up the auto-electrical division.

He looks younger.

I went and asked for it: that's how you got a job back then – see if they wanted you. I was in the spare parts section for six months, pedalling a bike all round Melbourne for them with a basket attachment at the front. You had to look neat. We were neat then – not like now. I got nine shillings and sixpence a week. Gave Mum the lot and she gave me two bob back. In those days the majority of your money went and you learnt to fight hard to budget.

After that I worked for thirteen years as a motor mechanic before I went into the police force.

I ask him how life had been for his family during the war years.

Mum was very concerned because she had family members stuck in Norwich in England during the bombing raids. Dad had a brother who served in the First World War. So, understandably, our family was worried about them. In those days the news was always a week old. These days you see war as it happens, on the telly. Back then you had to worry about what was really going on.

His voice levels out like a morning spent on a lake. There's no alarm in it; he's just explaining how life was.

Mum sent food parcels to relatives in England – things such as tea or cube sugar, and small packets of sultanas and raisins – it all had to do with food coupons: people swapped butter coupons for tea coupons, for example. Hessian sugarbags were used to cover the food parcels. People's addresses were written on white cloth and then their names were sewn onto the brown parcel bag.

The majority of our work at that time was for the United States Marine Corps, working on every conceivable type of truck and jeep. The vehicle would be jacked up and stripped from front to back for inspection. It couldn't have been a better schooling for apprentice mechanics. You did your apprentice-ship and that was that.

He sniffs satisfactorily, every millimetre the noble truck mechanic.

I left in '50, came back eighteen months later. I left there because S L Cheney's (they were the Vauxhall agents), offered ten bob a week more pay. I'd just got engaged and was looking for more money. You'd do your valve grinds. You just mechani-cally replaced things. They were heading towards automation. But automation doesn't have any feeling. When you personally tune up a vehicle, it hums.

He smiles and you just know what mechanics means to him. I think if we harnessed Ralph West's energy we'd get out of the rut we're in in Australia.

In '55, when I'd just turned twenty-eight, I went along to police recruitment and I got knocked back, because the age limit was *up to* twenty-eight and I was too old. A month later, the age was lifted to thirty and again I attended, but this time I was knocked back because I was overweight. So I went to Finlay's Gym. Did exercise. Skipping was involved. You did light weights, too. Also, I couldn't swim at the time. So I learnt swimming, knowing that I'd have to do lifesaving and so on.

I went back to the depot in '56 and did the medical in May. You did your medical first day. In the afternoon you sat for a written entrance exam. Next day you returned to see whether or not you were successful. Started as a recruit in the June of '56. On fourteen pound nineteen and sixpence a week.

'It must've felt like job security had finally arrived.'

It had to do with the permanency. That was the appointment. You're in it for life. I was keen.

'What was the attitude of the drill-instructors?'

In the police you need to be able to laugh. I suppose it's humour on the darker side.

They would say flattering things like 'Every time I see you blokes I believe in birth control.' (*Chuckles at the cruelty.*) You've got to be able to take that chiding. In the police you need to be able to laugh. I suppose it's humour on the darker side.

Joy gives us more coffee and we thank her. I'm addicted to the stuff. Ralph sips his thoughtfully, long fingers tapping on his face.

I was stationed first at Russell Street. Each day you were assigned a beat for that day. One of my beats was Parliament, in that area. Parliament was out of sessions a lot. No one came in over the gates, or anything like that. The greatest danger was the night shift – 11 pm till 7 am. My night shift was ten days straight, then you had your days off. You basically had your vagrant types, whom you'd come across sleeping in the gardens. (*His expanded arms indicate an army of dispossessed people.*) In winter they'd be bumping out of there, looking for somewhere warmer to sleep. I was at the old City Watch House. You arrested them for Drunk and Disorderly. The 'wet cell', we called where we put them, the bad ones. It had slats on the floor so they could wet through it. If they were ill you just rinsed the cell down. And some of them were violent. 'Make it hard for a young copper,' they seemed to be saying.

Stares off into space and the entirety of Doncaster.

But it was the security of the job you were after – as well as the camaraderie, the mateship. You had your squad mates. (*Opens his palms to reveal this physical and spiritual gift.*) Just normal things you loved, like going to work. Not everyone went to Russell Street. You were put into what was called a district. Some of them were seconded to Wireless Patrol. We lived in Reservoir at that time.

Six o'clock swill, then the pubs would empty out. 'Domestics', you'd go to. Having come from hard-times-but-happy, you'd go to where dinners'd been thrown into a wall three months ago. It's surprising how often alcohol's been involved in various unhappy situations, with either the perpetrator or the victim being affected by alcohol.

Stops, just stops. A few quizzical starlings stop, too, on the spouting of Ralph's roof. There are all sorts of fluttery pecky noises there.

In an instant you are in an entirely different world from that of the police station – from the intestines of the division van into a poor home. Front door is swinging open now. Mum comes out, carrying a baby in her arms. Her cardie is all undone and she's bare-breasted. Her drunken husband sinks the slipper into her back whilst she's clutching the baby and falling. This is right in front of you, in East Preston, like. I threw him in the back of the van straight away. I virtually couldn't understand it, myself. I said to him 'You're a brave sort of a gentleman. Do you want to have a go at me?' It was midnight or just after. You just write 'Too drunk to sign' on the charge sheet. They couldn't even wave a pen over the blurry paper. They'd probably be hit for five quid in those days.

In those days the Divvy van was shared between Northcote and Preston. One station provided the driver, the other the sub-officer.

The actuality of recollection is becoming more highly charged. Ralph is moving out of recollection into the present. More life is in him and he's talking differently, becoming less formal, opening up, giving up on etiquette for the uselessness of it. He's relaxed and relaxing.

You'd go to the 'domestic' where the children were cowering in the corner, frightened of Daddy. The police were more or less, well, they were expected to have a protective instinct, because of your concern for the welfare of children.

Fiddling with his elegant cloth tie. His fingers are huge.

There were certain families whose names cropped up on the Daily Circular. That was our official police publication. It showed you what offences had taken place. Missing people came out in the *Police Gazette*. I was stationed at Northcote for two and a half years – the then Mobile Traffic Section – after applying for a vacancy. There was a departmental form to apply for vacancies in *Police Orders*. I was a traffic cop in '59. Yes, you were a traffic man!

He shows me a photo album of several Ralphs astride flash motorbikes.

I was six and a half years on the bikes. (*He grins at the tremendous power and sheer beauty of them.*) I did the Gembrook fires, those bushfires they had up there in the early '60s. Up in The Dandies, you know. That again was just the Mobile Traffic Section. A lot of us went up there to help out. The first time I went there was on a motorbike – a Gold Star BSA – as a first constable.

He speaks now of death and the inevitability and commonality of it.

This was when I was with the accident investigation section. At later fires, the coroner said, looking at the charred bodies, 'Could anything have been done to prevent this sort of thing?' The keys had been in the ignition and all the cocks of the water tanker were still open. They'd utilised everything they had, to deal with it.

In 1956–57 at Christmas/New Year I did six weeks at the old Flinders Street extension morgue. From Russell Street I was rostered for duty at the morgue. We had an exhumed coffin which wasn't very pleasant odour-wise. At the same time a sixteen-month-old baby came in. It used to be common then to have harness straps around babies. With one of those on, it had stood up on the edge of its pram, then sat down and garrotted itself.

He is moving into horror, the real dutiful honest cop's lot, and it's the ease of familiarity here that offers good words.

The father, accompanied by two uncles, came in to identify the baby. He said 'Can I please hold my son?' I'd just taken him out of the fridge. I said to him 'Think of him as merely sleeping. Try and think of him just that way.' You find that helps, in tragic circumstances – just think of dead citizens asleep.

The father, accompanied by two uncles, came in to identify the baby. He said 'Can I please hold my son?' I'd just taken him out of the fridge. I said to him 'Think of him as merely sleeping. Try and think of him just that way.' You find that helps, in tragic circumstances – just think of dead citizens asleep.

He pleaded with me, this man. *'Please!'* He said again *'Please!'* He kissed the body on the forehead like this, see? (*Mimes a gentle man's loving kiss on a forehead – in his armchair, cradling a ghost, as it were.*) And said, 'Goodbye son!'

I'm afraid I had a thick throat at the time and couldn't possibly speak. Someone said 'He's had plenty of Relaxa-Tabs.' It was the loving father, from memory. He said 'Can you please put him in this clean clothing. My wife wants him buried in these clothes.'

Some hours later, Inspector Opperman, the duty officer, said 'How are you?' And I said back to him 'If you don't mind, Sir, I'm bloody awful!' After I said that to my superior officer, I was all right then. It got the emotional burden out of me, and I could then continue my duty.

He then just had a conversation with me about family matters. 'Wait till your baby is a teenager.' My own baby was thirteen months older than the dead baby. I had a horrific nightmare that night. I dreamed my own baby was waving bye-bye to me at the morgue. But I went to work as usual the next day.

He holds his throat, moves awkwardly, there's nowhere to go. But back to the stories.

I was in the Accident Squad for a while – a good while, actually. Fatal accidents were experienced on practically a daily basis. There was once this fellow, he sat on some railway lines intending to commit suicide and a truck ran over him! It's hard to believe but it's true. The truck hit him and carted him eighty-five metres up the road; nothing left of him. A constable at the scene was getting most upset. I said 'It just goes to show you. How stiff can you get? Here he was just waitin' for a train to come and a bloody truck cleans him up. Think about it son,' I said to him.

As you get older in the service you need to laugh as a sort of safety valve, as some pretty horrific things happen to you, all around you, in the job. When I did the lectures I showed photos and they were all rather gory. I said to these recruits 'What you're dealing with are your fellow humans. They can't hurt any more so far as this life is concerned. Think of them as dead meat. But give the dignity and respect you would want for yourself or your own loved ones. That way, you should be able to cope.

He scratches his thinning black hair.

The worst thing you must do is a death message. People always think the worst when they see the police there on the doorstep. All you can hope after your life's service in the police force is that you've made a difference. The victims? You've got regard for them. To take someone's liberty from them and slam the door on them is what justice is about. You've helped rid society of a menace.

It's the fact that the policeman respects law and order. You are the visible symbol of that. What rights does the ordinary John Citizen have? Their future? You're trying to make it better for them, during the trauma that the person's going through at the time.

A small boy had an obstruction of the throat once. We done a lifesaving flight from Mordialloc Bridge to escort him to the old Children's Hospital in Carlton. This was in the times before they had a master switch at D24 to turn all the traffic lights to green. It was a baby boy in a humidicrib. We had to wait for the name of the doctor and the child. Later the father embraced me and said, 'I can say nothing but thank you. All these men, for all these men who've helped us' We took the sick baby to the Children's Hospital. Fourteen minutes, it took. From Mordialloc to there. You never forget things like that.

To cap off his recollections, Ralph West tells me a story whose raw reality is almost impossible to bear.

In 1972, when I was with the Accident Investigation section, I was detailed to attend a fatal hit–run collision involving two pedestrians. Vicki, a fifteen-year-old high school student, was crossing Waverley Road, with her male companion, to meet her parents. Both young people were struck by a speeding car. The lad was thrown clear but had both legs shattered. Vicki was dragged eighty-five metres before being dislodged. She suffered horrendous injuries and died on the scene. The offending vehicle did not stop and continued on at high speed.

Vicki's parents were witnesses to this horrific collision, so statements had to be obtained from them. I was willing to wait, but Vicki's father asked that I call at their home the next day.

I honoured his request the next day, and a colleague and I took half an hour to get the statements. Needless to say, both parents were distraught after having retold what they saw. I felt I could not leave at that time and stayed to talk with them, especially Vicki's dad, for a further hour at least.

A few days later Vicki's dad had a heart attack. But despite this, and their grief, within a fortnight Vicki's dad had forwarded a letter of appreciation of our conduct to the Chief Commissioner. For that man, at that time, to forward such a letter gave me such a rich reward. It was a reward no money could buy, and I appreciated how fortunate I was to have met such wonderfully considerate people. The shame was the tragic circumstances which brought about this meeting.

He shows me the letter. It reads:

> *Dear Sir,*
>
> *Just recently my daughter was killed in a road accident and we subsequently received a visit from two members of the Accident Appreciation Squad.*
>
> *On behalf of my wife and myself I would like to place on record our deep and sincere appreciation of the manner in which these officers carried out what must be one of the most difficult duties in the Force.*
>
> *The men concerned were Sergeant West and Senior Constable Thomas and I can only say that they are a credit to the Victoria Police Force and indeed, would be a credit to any Force in the world.*
>
> *Sergeant West, in particular, showed a depth of compassion and understanding which is rare. He went beyond his line of duty in bringing comfort to my wife and myself at a time of our greatest sorrow.*
>
> *I will say no more, other than that these men command my greatest respect and admiration.*
>
> *Sincerely,*
>
> *V.T. Smith.*

He then finishes the story.

Policemen do not seek honour or reward for their service, but rewards such as that letter and, years later, that hug make all the disappointments, and sacrifices made over the years, more than worthwhile.

Vicki's dad had ongoing heart problems and, as a consequence, could not attend the inquest hearing or the later court proceedings against the driver concerned. I made a point of sitting next to Vicki's mother to comfort her as she relived that tragic night on hearing the evidence. After this I had no further contact with the family.

Twenty-three years later, when I was retired, I was attending a seminar for heart patients at Epworth Hospital. The co-ordinator spoke of, and to, a man present, who had a history of heart traumas and treatments. The man commented that his problems had started after witnessing a collision which killed his daughter.

During a break I asked this man if his daughter's name was Vicki, and I introduced myself. He looked at me, then broke into a huge smile. He embraced me, saying how great it was to see me again and how pleased Vicki's mother would be to hear from me, as they often spoke of me.

The last thing Ralph West tells me is this:

Policemen do not seek honour or reward for their service, but rewards such as that letter and, years later, that hug make all the disappointments, and sacrifices made over the years, more than worthwhile.

Also by Barry Dickins from

Hardie Grant Books

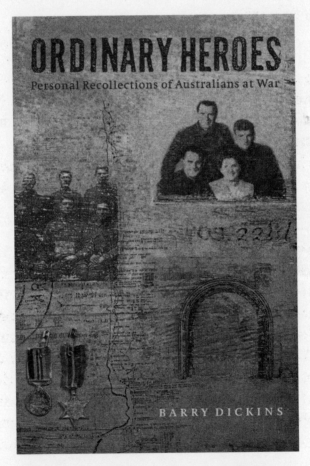

Bestseller in 1999
ISBN 1 86498 103 2

The Japanese men were silent. Gestured, they just gestured. made us walk toward the sea. We were a long line across the bay. They gradually shot with their rifles ... I got the bullet in the left side ... the water was only up to our knees ... I was too frightened to get up. So I stayed bobbing around in the water until the time when I absolutely had to get up. There was nothing to see. Everybody had been shot. The whole twenty-one of them.
Vivian Bullwinkle

When Parer shot this phota – you see it there? – we never knew a thing about it ... Why is this picture so famous? I wouldn't ... have ... a ... clue! Parer named it Comradeship.
Wal Johnson, Australian soldier immortalised by Cinesound war correspondent Damien Parer's famous photograph.

Ordinary Heroes is the result of a year on the road in a battered Kingswood, searching for memories of war. It records Barry Dickins' remarkably frank interviews with ordinary Australians who found themselves caught up in some of the most nightmarish events of the twentieth century. With them we go back to the trenches at Gallipoli, revisit the Burma–Thailand railway and experience the terror of being stranded in the jungles of Vietnam. These are tender stories from rather reluctant heroes who saw what they did as nothing more than duty.

ANF   A/363.20994/DIC..39100